Next in Line

The American Vice Presidency

Next in Line
The American Vice Presidency

By Barbara Silberdick Feinberg

Democracy in Action
Franklin Watts
A Division of Grolier Publishing
New York London Hong Kong Sydney
Danbury, Connecticut

*For my brother, Norman Silberdick Jr.,
and my nephews Aaron and Andrew*

Frontis: The United States Capitol

Photographs © copyright: Library of Congress
Photographs ©: AP/Wide World Photos: p. 136; Bettmann
Archive: pp. 29, 41, 57, 111; Corbis-Bettmann: pp. 60, 78, 103,
105, 142; Courtesy of Gerald R. Ford Library: p. 52; Hubert H.
Humphrey Photography Collection, Minnesota Historical Society:
p. 151; John F. Kennedy Library: p. 48; Library of Congress: p.
106; Lyndon Baines Johnson Library Collection: p. 116 (Cecil
Stoughton); National Graphic Center: p. 2; New York Public
Library Picture Collection: pp. 37, 83, 88; Reuters/Bettmann: p.
162; Rothco Cartoons: pp. 18 (Bill Mitchell), 161 (Wicks, The
Signal); Theodore Roosevelt Collection, Harvard College Library:
p. 109; UPI/Bettmann: pp. 16, 47, 67, 71, 114, 125, 129, 155;
UPI/Corbis-Bettmann: pp. 91, 146; Virginia Museum of Fine
Arts: p. 22; The White House: pp. 14, 140 (Phil Humnicky).

Library of Congress Cataloging-in-Publication Data
Feinberg, Barbara Silberdick.
Next in line: the American vice presidency/by Barbara Silberdick
Feinberg.
p.   cm. —(Democracy in action)
Includes bibliographical references and index.
Summary: A study of the office of the vice presidency, its origins,
history, responsibilities, and privileges; and an overview of the
individuals who have served in that office.
ISBN 0-531-11283-7
1. Vice-Presidents—United States—
History—Juvenile literature.
2. Vice-Presidents—United States—Juvenile literature.
[1. Vice-Presidents.] I. Title. II. Series: Democracy in action
(Franklin Watts, Inc.)
JK609.5.F45   1996
353.03'18—dc20   96-11617
                                                          CIP
                                                          AC

Contents

Acknowledgments
7

One
"His Superfluous Excellency":
Perspectives on the Vice Presidency
9

Two
A Constitutional Afterthought:
Creation of the Vice Presidency
20

Three
Filling the Number-Two Spot:
Selection of Vice Presidents
34

Four
A Rogues' Gallery:
Vice Presidential Scandals and Follies
54

Five
Politics Makes Strange Bedfellows:
Tensions Between Presidents and Vice Presidents
72

Six
Rising to the Occasion:
Succession to the Presidency
95

Seven
A Heartbeat Away: Vice Presidential Responses
to Presidential Disabilities
120

Eight
Being a Team Player:
The Expansion of Vice Presidential Duties
139

Nine
Reinventing the Government:
Proposals to Reform the Vice Presidency
164

Notes
175

Glossary
187

Bibliography
190

Appendix: Vice Presidents of the United States
194

Index
202

Acknowledgments

I WOULD LIKE TO THANK THE FOLLOWING PEOPLE FOR HELPING me locate information used in this book: Marilyn Bunshaft, Community Affairs Officer, East Meadow Public Library; Douglas L. Feinberg, Columbia College, class of 1995; Jeremy R. Feinberg, Columbia University School of Law, class of 1995; Suzanne Freedman, freelance researcher; Elizabeth Inglehart, attorney; and staff members of the office of the vice president.

I am especially grateful to my editor, Lorna Greenberg, not only for giving me the benefit of her superb professional skills but for offering me encouragement when I needed it most. I most appreciate the sharp mind and keen wit that my friend and neighbor, Jeanie Smart, offered me as I sought catchy chapter titles, and her willingness to read and comment on the first chapter even though she dislikes having to operate computers that feature a mouse. Once more, I am indebted to my college classmate and long-time friend, Gina Cane, for thinking up a title for this book when my mind went blank and for enduring with her usual patience and good humor my endless conversations about the book.

B.S.F.

"His Superfluous Excellency":
Perspectives on the Vice Presidency

I like it much better than service in the House or Senate. In the vice-presidency you have an opportunity to see the whole operation of the government and participate in its decisions.

Richard M. Nixon

THOMAS R. MARSHALL, WOODROW WILSON'S VICE PRESIdent, described the plight of the nation's second-leading citizen in the following story: "Once upon a time there was a farmer who had two sons. One of them ran away to sea, the other was elected Vice President of the United States. Nothing was heard of either of them again."[1] As the story suggests, the office has doomed many of its occupants to obscurity. For example, most Americans cannot identify George M. Dallas, Schuyler Colfax, and Charles W. Fairbanks; yet, they have left some traces. Dallas, Texas, Colfax, California, and Fairbanks, Alaska, honor these vice presidents. Similarly, many people do not know that the word "gerrymander" is derived from the name of Vice President Elbridge Gerry. In 1811, as governor of Massachusetts, Gerry signed a law permitting the boundaries of election districts to be readjusted in favor of the political party in power. The redistricting produced some oddly shaped voting divisions, resembling salamanders, which prompted use of the term gerrymander to describe their creation. The public is also generally unaware that Gerry was the only vice president to have signed the Declaration of Independence and served as a delegate to the Constitutional Convention. Two vice presidential names were deliberately lost to history when Jeremiah J. Colbath and Leslie King chose to be legally called Henry Wilson and Gerald Ford. Other vice presidents who kept the same name for life, William A. Wheeler, Thomas A. Hendricks, and Garret A. Hobart, may be even more unfamiliar to the public.

Only nine vice presidents out of the forty-five who have served won two terms in office: John Adams, George Clinton, Daniel Tompkins, John C. Calhoun, Thomas R. Marshall, John N. Garner, Richard M. Nixon, Spiro T. Agnew, and George Bush. What's more, few vice presidents moved to the presidency by election. John Adams and Martin Van Buren accomplished this feat, but 152 years passed before it was duplicated by George Bush. In 1800, two former vice presidents, John Adams and Thomas Jefferson, were opponents in the race for president, but 168 years elapsed before two of their successors, Hubert H. Humphrey and Richard M. Nixon, competed in a presidential election.

During eighteen administrations, for a total of almost thirty-eight years, the government managed to muddle through without the services of a vice president because the incumbent had died, resigned, or succeeded to the presidency. The vice presidency was held in such low esteem that often the only politicians willing to be elected to the office were either old or in poor health. In one case, William Rufus DeVane King, the nation's only bachelor vice president, died of tuberculosis in 1853, six weeks after his inauguration, and never even got to serve with President Franklin Pierce. King took the oath of office in Cuba, where he had gone to restore his fading health, and became the only vice president to be sworn in outside the country. In 1912, William Howard Taft's vice president, James S. Sherman, received three and a half million votes in his bid for a second term although he had died a week before the presidential election was held. The problem of vice presidential vacancies wasn't remedied until ratification of the Twenty-fifth Amendment in 1967, which suggests that the vice president may have been considered one of the more dispensable officials in government.

For most of the nineteenth and part of the twentieth century, vice presidents were unable to make names for themselves. There wasn't much for them to do, and what they did do—preside over the Senate and cast tie-breaking votes—lacked the drama and excitement needed to produce headlines. Only when presidents died in office— six times before the 1940s—did people pay any attention to their vice presidents, and then only because they were presidential successors. Modern historians give the nineteenth-century replacement presidents John Tyler and Millard Fillmore below-average ratings, consider Andrew Johnson a failure, and rank Chester Alan Arthur as average. Theodore Roosevelt, from the turn of the century, is classified as near great, and Calvin Coolidge, who took over in 1923, falls below average.[2] Roosevelt and Coolidge—the best and the worst—were elected to the presidency in their own right afterwards.

The office of vice president was even treated as an object of ridicule. In their Pulitzer Prize–winning 1931 musical comedy, *Of Thee I Sing*, George and Ira Gershwin caricatured the vice presidency by creating the person of the bumbling, inept Alexander Throttlebottom, who could gain entrance to the White House only by joining a guided tour. They were not the first to regard the vice president as a buffoon. According to a story that still circulates, in the early days of the republic, one senator mocked the office by proposing to give the vice president of the United States the title "His Superfluous Excellency."[3]

A more popular form of address, "the Veep," gained currency in the second half of the twentieth century as the vice presidency underwent a major transformation. In 1948, Alben W. Barkley's young grandson, Stephen Pruitt, thought the words "vice president" were a mouthful and coined the term "veep" to show his respect as well as his affection for his grandfather, Harry Truman's victorious running mate.[4] The term became part of the national vocabulary of politics. The nickname's survival not only illustrates the American preference for abbreviation, but also suggests that, unlike their predecessors, more recent vice presidents have left a mark on American politics.

What has led to this change has been the increased visibility and competence of vice presidents in a changing world. No longer are they consigned to oblivion, the fate of most of the successors of John Adams and Thomas Jefferson. They now live in an age in which the federal government is expected to accept greater responsibility for the public well-being and to assume leadership of a postwar free world threatened by a nuclear stalemate and widespread international tensions. In this altered context, vice presidents have repeatedly demonstrated their willingness to assist the president as spokespeople for the administration. They have acted as partisan campaigners, ceremonial dignitaries, traveling goodwill ambassadors, and as advisors. In addition to their senatorial duties, they now participate in discussions of domestic policy and national security. Richard M. Nixon put it succinctly: "I like it much better than service in the House or Senate. In the vice-presidency you have an opportunity to see the whole operation of the government and participate in its decisions."[5] It is doubtful that any nineteenth-century vice president could have made that claim.

According to the authors of the Twentieth Century Fund Task Force on the vice presidency, "Although the vice president, like the co-pilot of a jumbo jet, is not in command of the plane, the vice president is there to assist the president in the discharge of his duties, and he is ready to assume the controls whenever it becomes necessary to do so. Like the co-pilot, the vice president may never be called upon to 'fly the plane,' but it is comforting to know that he is there to do so if the need arises."[6]

Over the last sixty or so years, vice presidents have been called upon to step in and take charge during national tragedies, such as the death of President Franklin D. Roosevelt, the assassination of President John F. Kennedy, and the resignation of President Nixon. Of the three vice presidents who replaced them, historians rate Harry S. Truman as near great, Lyndon B. Johnson as above average, Gerald Ford as average.[7] Truman and Johnson were subsequently elected to full terms as president. They had proven themselves under the most trying circumstances. Unlike their predecessors, modern vice presidents have quietly assumed the reins of government when presidents became disabled, actions given further legitimacy by the passage of the Twenty-fifth Amendment. The competent way Nixon handled matters during President Dwight D. Eisenhower's illnesses and George Bush dealt with the assassination attempt on and illnesses of President Ronald W. Reagan won the two vice presidents personal accolades and greater respect for the office they occupied.

The trappings of the vice presidential office have changed as responsibilities have been added. While vice presidents were always accorded a nineteen-gun

This hundred-year-old Victorian house on the grounds of the Naval Observatory has been the vice president's residence since 1975.

salute, they failed to receive any substantial perks of office until the mid-1970s. At that time, the Admiral's House at the Naval Observatory was converted into an official residence for vice presidents and their families. Previously, they had lived in hotel rooms or, if they could afford it, rented temporary homes in the Washington area. Better airplanes were designated to serve as "Air Force Two." The official seal of office was redesigned to reflect an elevation of the vice president's status. The eagle at rest was replaced by an eagle with its wings extended, a cluster of stars around its head, and a claw full of arrows. More importantly, instead of borrowing assistants from the president and other government agencies, vice presidents were given sufficient funding to hire their own support staff to handle the press, write speeches, and schedule appointments; political staff to look out for their interests; and policy staff to help develop proposals to be brought to the president's attention. In the 1790s, John Adams had received a salary of $5,000 while George Washington was given $25,000; but by 1995, Vice President Albert Gore was paid $171,500 and $10,000 for expenses, and President Bill Clinton received $200,000 plus $170,000 for expenses.[8]

Unlike their predecessors, modern vice presidents have been free to declare their candidacy for the presidency without fear of antagonizing the presidents they serve because the Twenty-second Amendment, approved in 1951, has limited incumbent presidents to two terms. Richard M. Nixon, Hubert H. Humphrey, Walter F. Mondale, and George Bush were nominated as their parties' standard-bearers as soon as they completed their vice presidential terms. Only Bush won election right away; Nixon had to wait and run again eight years later before he succeeded. The others went down to defeat, although their losses at the polls were more a reflection of the political climate than of doubts about their qualifications for office.

As a group, the vice presidents of the United States have been just a little more representative of the diversity of the American people than the presidents—but that is not saying much. Charles G. Curtis, who served with President Herbert C. Hoover, was the only vice president who could claim a Native American heritage. He was one-quarter Kaw Indian. No African Americans or Latinos have as yet been chosen as vice presidential nominees, but in 1984, Democratic presidential candidate Walter F. Mondale chose a woman, Geraldine Ferraro, a member of Congress from New York, for the second slot on the ticket. This was the first time a woman had received the vice presidential nomination of a major American political party. She brought to the campaign feistiness and ethnic appeal, as well as experience in politics.

*W*hen *Nelson Rockefeller took office as vice president in 1975, he decided the eagle in the vice president's seal (top) looked like a wounded quail, and had the seal redesigned (bottom).*

Ferraro's was not the only candidacy to demonstrate that change is possible. After 1960, when John F. Kennedy, a Catholic, was elected president, other Catholics were nominated for vice president, including Sargent Shriver, who ran in 1972 with Senator George McGovern of South Dakota. Perhaps the political parties will soon welcome members of other groups who by tradition were not thought to be acceptable national candidates.

Despite their relative obscurity for the first hundred-odd years of the republic, American vice presidents have been a rather impressive lot, well qualified to serve as second in command. Thirty-four of the forty-five attended college. Thirty-two were trained as lawyers, four were bankers, and three were news editors or reporters. Among the six businessmen were millionaires but also a tailor (Andrew Johnson), a shoemaker (Henry Wilson), and the proprietor of a men's clothing store that failed (Harry S. Truman), so at least a few vice presidents had faced the same difficulties as those of ordinary citizens and had a personal understanding of their problems. About a third of the vice presidents joined the military as young men. Collectively, their service records extend from the French and Indian War to Vietnam, although none fought in the Korean War. Six vice presidents were veterans of World War II (Richard Nixon, Lyndon Johnson, Hubert Humphrey, Spiro Agnew, Gerald Ford, George Bush).

The nation's forty-five vice presidents have brought a wealth of experience to the job. Fourteen had served as governors of their state, twenty-four had been members of the House of Representatives, and twenty had been United States senators. Twelve had represented their country as diplomats, while three had been appointed members of the Cabinet: Secretary of State Thomas Jefferson, Secretary of War John C. Calhoun, and Secretary of Agriculture Henry A. Wallace. Another, Charles G. Dawes, was the first director of the budget and the only vice president to win a Nobel Peace Prize.

The vice presidents have come from a total of twenty states. Eighteen made their homes in the North, thirteen came from the South, another thirteen hailed from the Midwest, but only one had roots on the West Coast. New York has contributed the most vice presi-

*A political cartoonist presented the
nomination of Geraldine Ferraro for the office
of vice president as a milestone in the progress of
women toward full political equality.*

dents of any state, with a total of eleven, perhaps because for a long time it had the most votes to be cast
in elections. Next has been Indiana, which prompted
one native son, Vice President Marshall, to quip that
the reason so many Hoosiers became vice president
was that the state produced many "first-rate second-
rate men."[9]

Following this overview of the vice presidency,
Chapter Two offers the strange tale of how the framers
of the Constitution made a last-minute decision to create the vice presidency. Chapter Three examines the
convoluted constitutional and political mechanisms for
choosing vice presidential candidates, including the
peculiar case of unelected vice presidents. Chapter
Four takes up one drawback of the selection process,
notorious vice presidents whose fitness for office was
compromised by scandal. Chapter Five discusses
another consequence of the selection process, mis-

18

matched vice presidents who found themselves constantly at odds with the presidents they served. Chapter Six explains what happened when haphazardly elected and often unprepared vice presidents suddenly had to take over the leadership of the nation as replacement presidents. Chapter Seven looks at the vice presidents' conduct during presidential disabilities and the effect of the Twenty-fifth Amendment on their behavior. Chapter Eight offers a survey of vice presidents who became team players and traces the development of their extra-constitutional responsibilities. Chapter Nine concludes with a discussion of various proposals to eliminate or reform the office of vice president.

A Constitutional Afterthought:
Creation of the Vice Presidency

My country in its wisdom contrived for me the most insignificant office that ever the invention of man contrived or his imagination conceived. . . .

John Adams

DURING THE SWELTERING SUMMER OF 1787, FIFTY-FIVE DELE-gates assembled in Philadelphia, representing all the former American colonies except Rhode Island, which declined to participate. They came together to strengthen and reform the ineffective government of the United States, but they soon abandoned this project. Instead, they embarked on a series of extensive discussions and debates and carefully crafted a number of compromises to create a new, more powerful government. Far from their minds was any thought of the vice presidency, as they began to draft the main outlines of the Constitution.

There were, however, ample precedents for a vice presidency. Five states already had lieutenant governors who acted as governor when needed. In New York, the lieutenant governor presided over the State Senate and cast tie-breaking votes. Yet, the existence of these

20

state officials escaped the delegates' attention. In fact, there might never have been a vice president of the United States at all, were it not for three issues that remained unresolved as the Constitutional Convention drew to a close: a method of electing the president; the method of selection of the presiding officer of the Senate; and a plan for filling presidential vacancies.

Throughout the Constitutional Convention, the delegates failed to agree upon a method of electing the president of the United States. Representatives from small states, including Roger Sherman of Connecticut and Charles Pinckney of South Carolina, opposed direct election by the people, a plan favored by James Madison of Virginia and Gouverneur Morris and James Wilson of Pennsylvania. The plan's opponents feared that the populous states would have too much influence over the outcome of presidential elections. For similar reasons, they objected to selection by Congress, the method initially accepted by most delegates, since seats in the House of Representatives were to be allocated according to the number of residents in each state. That proposal presented additional difficulties because it could make executives too dependent on or beholden to the legislators who voted them into office. In June, mention was made of a plan to have electors, chosen by the people in each state, select a president, but at this time, the idea was too novel to be taken seriously. During the same month, mention of a vice president was made for the first time. Alexander Hamilton presented an elaborate outline of a new government, including a president chosen by electors and serving for life. He offered that:

> The President of the Senate shall be vice President of the United States. On the death, resignation, impeachment, removal from office, or absence from the United States, of the President thereof, the Vice

21

An artist's view of George Washington addressing the Constitutional Convention

President shall exercise all the powers by this Constitution vested in the President, until another shall be appointed, or until he shall return within the United States.[1]

The delegates never discussed Hamilton's plan.

In votes taken in July and August, presidential election by Congress again won reluctant support until the delegates tried to work out the details of the selection process. At that point, differences between the large and small states surfaced once more. To avoid a stalemate, Roger Sherman came up with a suggestion. During an earlier disagreement over apportionment of seats in Congress, he had negotiated the Connecticut Compromise, giving small states equal representation with the large states in the Senate and allotting seats in the House on the basis of population. On August 31,

Sherman proposed that the issue of selecting a president be turned over to the Committee of Eleven, also known as the Committee on Postponed Matters, an apt title.

In four days, the committee came up with a compromise solution to the problem: an electoral-college system. Electors selected in each of the states would choose the president. The president had to receive a majority of the electoral votes in order to be declared the winner. To prevent electors from voting exclusively for local favorites, each would cast two votes for president, one for a candidate outside their state. According to delegate James Wilson, the double vote would also prevent corruption and attempts to fix an election because both ballots would have equal weight.[2] As an additional incentive to make the second vote count, the committee decided to award the runner-up in the election a national office, the vice presidency.

During the convention's debate on this proposal, delegate Nathaniel Gorham of Massachusetts anticipated the future when he complained that "a very obscure man with very few votes may arrive at the appointment."[3] Later, Hugh Williamson of North Carolina observed that "such an officer as vice-President was not wanted. He was introduced only for the sake of a valuable mode of election which required two to be chosen at the same time."[4] Nevertheless, the committee's proposal for electing a president and vice president was accepted. Unlike the president, the vice president did not have to be elected by a majority of the electoral votes cast. The Constitution's framers did provide that if the highest runners-up for vice president were tied, the Senate would choose between them. If no presidential candidate received a majority of electoral votes, the House of Representatives, with each state accorded one vote, would make the choice among the leading five candidates.

The office of vice president also gave the delegates a solution to the problem of choosing a presiding officer for the Senate. Tradition decreed that presiding officers voted only to break a tie. If a senator had been selected for this post, the senator's state would be represented by only one lawmaker for most issues. Alternatively, were the presiding officer to be given a vote, the state would be overrepresented in the Senate. The Committee on Postponed Matters proposed to make the new vice president the president of the Senate, voting only to end a tie. The vice president would preside at all impeachment trials (to remove national officials from office) held in the Senate except that of the president of the United States, when the chief justice would preside.

During the debate on this part of the Committee of Eleven's report, Delegate Elbridge Gerry of Massachusetts objected to giving the vice president a legislative post because it violated the guiding principle of the Constitution, separation of powers. "The close intimacy that must subsist between the President & vice-president makes it absolutely improper."[5] His views were supported by George Mason of Virginia, who thought the vice presidency was "an encroachment on the rights of the Senate; and that it mixed too much the Legislative & Executive, which as well as the Judiciary department, ought to be kept as separate as possible."[6] Delegate Sherman defended the plan on practical grounds. "If the vice-President were not to be President of the Senate, he would be without employment. . . ."[7]

In addition, the vice presidency provided the answer to another problem that had vexed the delegates, presidential succession. The Constitutional Convention had paid little attention to this issue until August, when the delegates' Committee on Detail recommended that in the event of a president's death or disability, the presiding officer of the Senate assume the president's duties. A debate on the proposal revealed widespread dissatisfaction over a possible breach of separation of powers. Alternative replacements, including the chief justice of the United States, the nation's highest judge, were suggested and voted down. Finally, the matter was referred to the Committee on Postponed Matters. The committee proposed that in the event of a presidential death, resignation, absence, or inability, the vice president take on the powers and duties of the presidency until a new president was chosen or the inability was removed.

During debates on this section of the committee's report, delegate Edmund Randolph of Virginia offered a separate proposal to empower Congress to designate presidential successors by law, in the event that both the president and vice president were unable to complete their terms of office.[8] Madison amended this proposal so that an interim official would hold office only until the president could resume the responsibilities or a new president was chosen. Madison preferred to have Congress call for special elections to fill a presidential vacancy, and to let presidential successors serve as acting presidents.[9] Like Madison, most of the delegates thought of the vice president as a temporary caretaker, not as a replacement intended to complete the remainder of a president's term.[10]

When the Committee of Style produced Article II, section 1, paragraph 6 in the final draft of the Constitution, the Committee on Postponed Matters clause was inadvertently combined with Randolph's measure. This created an ambiguous situation that the framers, eager to return home, overlooked:

> *In Case of the Removal of the President from Office, or of his Death, Resignation, or Inability to discharge the Powers and Duties of the said Office, the same shall devolve on the Vice President, and the*

Congress may by Law provide for the Case of Removal, Death, Resignation, or inability, both of the President and Vice President, declaring what Officer shall then act accordingly until the Disability be removed, or a President shall be elected. [emphasis added]

To what did the word "same" refer? If a president did not complete a term, did the vice president take over the office and become president or just assume the powers and duties and serve as an acting president? Was a vice president expected to complete a deceased president's full term, or to remain only until a special election could be held to fill the presidential vacancy? These issues would raise serious constitutional problems for the first vice president to fill a presidential vacancy. Other questions would arise when presidents became disabled. Who would determine their inability to perform their duties? Who would decide when they were capable of assuming their responsibilities once again?

Debates in the states about ratifying, or approving, the Constitution echoed arguments heard at the Convention, and the states, too, devoted little attention to the office of the vice president. Delegates to state ratifying conventions who disapproved of the vice presidency most frequently objected to the merging of executive and legislative functions. For example, in North Carolina, clergyman David Caldwell argued that "the Vice-President is made part of the legislative body, although there was an express declaration, that all the legislative powers were vested in the Senate and the House of Representatives."[11] Others who echoed his sentiments included Governor, later Vice President, George Clinton of New York, and soon-to-be senator Richard Henry Lee, future president James Monroe, and former delegate George Mason from Virginia.

Among the supporters of the new constitutional arrangement was Governor Samuel Johnston of North Carolina, who reasoned that "if one of the Senate was to be appointed Vice President, the state which he represented would either lose a vote if he was not permitted to vote on every occasion, or if he was, he might, in some sense have two votes."[12] Delegate James Madison of Virginia pointed out: "There is much more propriety in giving this office to a person chosen by the people at large, than to one of the Senate. . . . "[13] The most enduring defense of the office of vice presidency is in *Federalist Paper #68*, where Alexander Hamilton wrote:

> *The appointment of an extraordinary person, as Vice-President, has been objected to as superfluous, if not mischievous. . . . But two considerations seem to justify the ideas of the Convention in this respect. One is, that to secure at all times the possibility of a definitive resolution of the body, it is necessary that the President should have only a casting vote. And to take the Senator of any State from his seat as Senator, to place him as President of the Senate, would be to exchange, in regard to the State from which he came, a constant for a contingent vote. The other consideration is, that, as the Vice-President may occasionally become a substitute for the President. . . .* [14]

Only ten states participated in the nation's first presidential election under the new Constitution in 1789. North Carolina and Rhode Island had not yet ratified the document, and the New York State Assembly and Senate could not agree on a common method for choosing presidential electors. In five states, the legislatures designated electors, three states relied on popular election, while the remaining states combined the two methods.[15] Virginian George Washington won the election of 1789 with sixty-nine electoral votes while John Adams of Massachusetts was the highest runner-up, receiving thirty-four votes.

A short, dumpy-looking man, Vice President Adams, at age fifty-three, was awkward, tactless, and hypersensitive to criticism, an odd collection of qualities for a public official. He was also a man of principle, learning, and integrity. Early in his career he had defended British soldiers accused of killing civilians during the Boston Massacre and had gone on to serve in the Continental Congress before ten years of duty as an American diplomat in France, the Netherlands, and Great Britain. Determined to be an activist vice president, Adams set a standard that no later vice president has matched. Unlike his successors, he was a dominant figure in the upper house of the legislature, but the first Senate had only twenty-six members and was not yet well organized. When he assumed his responsibilities on April 21, he refused to become a silent ceremonial dignitary, claiming, "Not wholly without experience in public assemblies, I have been more accustomed to take a share in their debates than to preside over their deliberations."[16] During his first year as presiding officer of the Senate, Adams participated in debates, lecturing members and voicing his own opinions. He also helped to set the agenda of topics for discussion.

As vice president, Adams led the Senate on a month-long discussion of titles and addresses to enhance the dignity and authority of the new government and to accord it respect. He had been horrified by Shays's Rebellion, a violent tax protest by Massachusetts farmers in 1786. It confirmed his lack of confidence in the judgment of ordinary citizens, who, he feared, were more often guided by passions than reason.[17] He wanted government to be strong enough to check impulsive and destructive outbursts. This is why his concern with conferring titles was not as frivolous as it might appear. Since titles would command respect

John Adams, the nation's first vice president

and heighten the authority of the new government, Adams wanted the president to be addressed as "His Highness, the President of the United States of America and Protector of the Rights of the Same." A number of senators found Adams's preoccupation with titles ridiculous. William Maclay of Pennsylvania expounded at length on the meaning of "highness" as "the excess of stature," while Ralph Izard of South Carolina mockingly dubbed Adams "His Rotundity,"[18] an accurate albeit cruel reference to the vice president's well-rounded figure. Representative James Madison felt that Adams's proposal would be "dangerous to republicanism while George Washington found the whole issue ridiculous."[19] Under Madison's leadership, the title became simply, the president of the United States.

Arriving in New York, the nation's temporary capital, George Washington was inaugurated as president on

April 30, 1789. Plans for this ceremony had driven Adams to become even more obsessed with matters of ritual and procedure. There were no guidelines to govern the interactions of the president and Congress, or to determine how relations between the two houses of Congress should be conducted. Adams was concerned about his official status when George Washington entered the Senate chamber to be sworn in.

> *I feel great difficulty in how to act. I am possessed of two separate powers; the one is* esse *and the other is* posse. *I am Vice-President. In this I am nothing, but I may be everything. But I am president also of the Senate. When the President comes into the Senate, what shall I be?* [20]

Senator Oliver Ellsworth of Connecticut quickly checked the Constitution and assured the anxious vice president that "wherever the Senate are to be, there, sir, you must be the head of them."[21] Adams raised a number of other questions about etiquette, the rules of proper conduct. Should the senators be standing or seated when the president addressed them? How should the vice president behave? As bothersome as Adams was, in the opinion of the Senate, he did force the members to establish rules and procedures; but much of the pomp and formality that Adams demanded was dropped by Thomas Jefferson some years later, when he became president.

Because the Constitution did not contain a vice presidential oath of office, Adams had to wait to be sworn in until Congress created one for him, and George Washington signed it into law. It has since been changed from a simple promise to support the Constitution of the United States, reminiscent of the presidential pledge, to a more elaborate statement:

I do solemnly swear (or affirm) that I will support and defend the Constitution of the United States against all enemies, foreign and domestic; that I will bear true faith and allegiance to the same; that I take this obligation freely, without any mental reservation or purpose of evasion; and that I will well and faithfully discharge the duties of the office on which I am about to enter. So help me God.[22]

Of course, Adams had been performing the duties of vice president long before he was officially installed in office.

While the first Congress had little difficulty voting a salary of twenty-five thousand dollars for the president of the United States, the issue of the vice president's remuneration set off a heated debate. Representative Alexander White of Virginia argued that compensation should be based on the actual number of days the vice president spent presiding over the Senate because the Constitution "has not one syllable with respect to the pay of the Vice President." Representative Joshua Seney of Maryland wanted the vice president to be paid per diem, as the representatives were, because there was no way to compel his attendance in the Senate and he could "absent himself the whole time."[23] Virginia representative John Page came to the vice president's defense, insisting, "but as we have got him, we must maintain him."[24] James Madison's plea was both practical and eloquent. "If he is to be considered as the apparent successor of the President, to qualify himself the better for that office, he must withdraw from his other avocations, and direct his attention to the obtaining of a perfect knowledge of his intended business."[25] In other words, the vice president was to be one of the first recipients of a federal grant for on-the-job training, and finally the representatives voted for an annual salary of five thousand dollars.

In the presidential election of 1792, George Washington had not expressed a preference for any candidate. "Whosoever shall be found to enjoy the confidence of the States so far as to be elected Vice-President, cannot be disagreeable to me in that office."[26] Adams won a second term as vice president with seventy-seven electoral votes to New Yorker George Clinton's fifty. Alexander Hamilton, the nation's first secretary of the Treasury, had promoted Clinton's unsuccessful candidacy. Disqualified by foreign birth from becoming president himself, Hamilton wanted to play a major role in determining the nation's next president when Washington retired. He had not wanted his political rival, John Adams, to stake a claim on the presidency by winning reelection as vice president.

After his victory, Adams expressed his disillusionment with the vice presidency in a letter to his wife, complaining that "my country in its wisdom contrived for me the most insignificant office that ever the invention of man contrived or his imagination conceived. . . . I can do neither good nor evil."[27] Nevertheless, he continued to play a more important role in government than most of his successors would. During his eight years in office, he cast a record twenty-nine tie-breaking votes as the presiding officer of the Senate, the first successfully defending the president's power to remove an official from his administration. In view of Adams's experience in international relations, George Washington often consulted him on diplomatic matters. Adams also sat in on cabinet meetings and was invited to meet with the cabinet when Washington went out of town. After Adams, the vice president's active participation in foreign policy would fall into eclipse until the 1930s. It wasn't until President Woodrow Wilson took office that a vice president again held cabinet meetings when a president was absent.

The vice president may have been a constitutional afterthought, but the framers of the Constitution expected candidates for the second-highest elective office in the nation to be talented leaders, qualified to be president. Their expectations were realized when Adams and then Thomas Jefferson became vice president, but later elections proved disappointing. The office no longer attracted such outstanding public figures. This happened because the framers had not anticipated the rise of political parties, which complicated the electoral process and ultimately changed the way the number-two spot would be filled.

Filling the Number-Two Spot: Selection of Vice Presidents

I can see nothing whatever in the vice presidency for me. It would be an irksome, wearisome place.

Theodore Roosevelt

A NUMBER OF PROBLEMS HAVE ARISEN DURING THE PROCESS OF choosing the nation's vice presidents. The original electoral-college system outlined by the framers of the Constitution proved to be flawed: first, when it produced a president and vice president from different political parties, John Adams and Thomas Jefferson; and second, when it created a tie for the presidency between members of the same political party, Thomas Jefferson and Aaron Burr. The Twelfth Amendment to the Constitution (1804) corrected these defects but failed to prevent other serious complications, including the situation of a president and vice president who were personally or politically incompatible, like John Quincy Adams and John C. Calhoun, or James Garfield and Chester A. Arthur. The Twenty-fifth Amendment provided a plan to fill vice presidential vacancies, but created other difficulties including giving the public an unelected president, Gerald Ford, and an unelected vice president, Nelson A. Rockefeller (see Chapter 3).

Originally, the Constitution provided that each elector would cast two ballots for president, at least one of which had to be for a candidate from outside the elector's home state. The highest runner-up in the presidential election automatically became vice president. This did not present a problem until the 1790s, when differences over government policies spurred the development of rival political parties, the Federalists and the Democratic-Republicans, who offered opposing sets of candidates for president and vice president. Party leaders then began to manipulate the cumbersome electoral machinery to settle intraparty and interparty rivalries.

A famous intraparty power struggle took place during the election of 1796. Federalist John Adams's presidential candidacy was virtually assured since he had been Washington's vice president for two terms. His running mate was Thomas Pinckney of South Carolina. Opposing them was a slate of Democratic-Republicans, Thomas Jefferson of Virginia and Aaron Burr of New York. Federalist leader Alexander Hamilton, never a fan of Adams and his competitor for control of the party, saw an opportunity to use the electoral machinery to foil Adams's presidential aspirations. He connived to make Pinckney president instead. He encouraged electors in the northern states to give equal support to Adams and Pinckney, assuming that southern electors would not vote for Adams, a citizen of Massachusetts, but would find Pinckney acceptable and give him enough votes to elect him president. The northern electors, however, did not follow Hamilton's reasoning and cast eighteen of their ballots for other Federalist candidates. Pinckney was left with only fifty-nine votes, mostly from the South. As a result, Adams won the presidency with seventy-one votes, and Jefferson, as the runner-up with sixty-eight, became vice president. Hamilton's maneuvers produced a president and vice president from opposing political parties. One flaw in the electoral system had been exposed. To correct it, an amendment to separate the election of president and vice president was offered in Congress in 1797, but no action was taken.

Another flaw was revealed in the election of 1800. If loyal electors voted both ballots for their party's ticket, they risked a tie between their presidential and vice presidential candidates. To prevent this, party leaders arranged to have some electors abstain or withhold their second votes to get the desired outcome: a majority vote for their presidential nominee and a second-place finish for their vice presidential choice. This is why the Federalist ticket of John Adams and Charles C. Pinckney of South Carolina, Thomas's elder brother, mustered sixty-five and sixty-four votes respectively. The Democratic-Republicans' plans, however, went awry. Confusion about who was to withhold votes led the party's conscientious electors to give Jefferson and Burr seventy-three votes each. Because of the unexpected tie between Democratic candidates, other constitutional procedures came into play. The election was thrown into the House of Representatives, where Federalists, many of them defeated in the 1800 November elections, remained in control of the legislature until March, when the newly elected government would be sworn in. (In 1933, the Twentieth Amendment changed the swearing-in date to January, thus shortening the term of a "lame-duck" Congress.)

With each state given one vote, the lawmakers set about deciding who would serve as the next president of the United States. Voting in the House began on February 11, 1800, and went on for seven days and

Thomas Jefferson, the country's second vice president

thirty-six more ballots because Jefferson failed to receive the constitutionally required majority of votes. Many die-hard Federalists in the House hated Jefferson so much that they backed Burr, who did nothing to discourage them. As the balloting continued, Alexander Hamilton worked behind the scenes to undermine Jefferson's running mate, writing to his friends in Congress, "I trust that the Federalists will not finally be so mad as to vote for Burr. I speak with an intimate and accurate knowledge of character. His elevation can only promote the purposes of the desperate and profligate."[1] Burr and Hamilton had long been rivals in New York politics. Finally, Federalist representative James Bayard of Delaware informed the members of his party of his fears that further delays would cause a constitutional crisis.[2] After receiving assurances that the Democratic-Republicans would not completely dismantle Federalist programs or dismiss government employees purely for partisan reasons, he withheld his vote while Burr supporters from Maryland, South Carolina, and Vermont cast blank ballots, giving Jefferson the needed nine-state majority to become president.

Something had to be done to prevent future electoral stalemates. In 1802, the House approved a constitutional amendment to separate the election of the president and vice president, but the Senate could not muster the two-thirds vote needed for passage. Among others, Federalist senator Gouverneur Morris of New York defended the original method of election saying that it was "the mode least favorable to intrigue and corruption. . . ."[3] In the fall of 1803, the amendment was introduced again over a number of objections to the change. Senator Samuel White of Delaware cautioned that in choosing a vice presidential candidate, "The question will not be asked, is he capable? Is he honest? But can he by his name, by his connexions [sic], by his wealth, by his local situation, by his influence, or his intrigues best promote the election of a President?"[4] Nevertheless, the amendment passed the House 84–42 and the Senate 22–10.[5] By late September 1804, it had won approval from the necessary three-fourths of the states.

Unlike the original provisions of the Constitution, the amendment required the vice president to receive a majority of the votes cast in order to win election to office. In addition, it specified that in the event of a vice presidential tie, the Senate would select the winner from the two leading candidates. In 1836, Martin Van Buren's running mate, Richard M. Johnson, received 147 electoral votes, one vote short of the required majority, and became, by a vote of 33–14, the only vice president to be elected by the Senate.[6] In the case of a presidential tie, the amendment reduced the House's choice from the top five vote-getters to the top three. It also applied the same presidential qualifications of age, citizenship, and residence to the vice president. Finally, the amendment provided that if the House was unable to choose a president before the outgoing president's term expired, the new vice president would become president.

Once the separate election of the vice president was introduced, the quality of vice presidential nominees declined. After all, they no longer had a chance to be elected president. Throughout the remainder of the nineteenth century, the office attracted a number of second-rate politicians, with the exception of Jackson's vice president, Martin Van Buren. Some vice presidents were even plagued by scandal (see Chapter 4). So low did the position fall in public esteem, that many outstanding statesmen declined to serve. When approached to become the Whig party's vice presidential nominee in 1848, Daniel Webster remarked, "I do not propose to be buried until I am dead."[7]

Many vice presidents were ailing and old, seeking the position as a sinecure after a long, if not always distinguished, political career. Typical was Madison's first vice president, former governor George Clinton of New York, whom Senator William Plumer of New Hampshire described as follows: "He is old, feeble & altogether uncapable of the duty of presiding in the Senate. He has no mind—no intellect—no memory. He forgets the question—mistakes it—& not infrequently declares a vote before it is taken. . . ."[8] Given such officeholders, it was not surprising that six vice presidents died of natural causes before completing their terms: George Clinton, Elbridge Gerry, William R. King, Henry Wilson, Thomas A. Hendricks, and Garret A. Hobart.

With the growth of political parties and the development of the presidential nominating convention in the 1830s, the selection of a vice president soon became subject to political wheeling and dealing, much as opponents of the Twelfth Amendment had feared. Through most of the nineteenth and the first half of the twentieth century, political bosses routinely picked vice presidential candidates for their parties. The bosses were party leaders who controlled a bloc of delegates and their votes. Their power was based in state or local government where they proffered jobs, contracts for public works, and other services or favors, in exchange for votes. One of the earliest bosses was Martin Van Buren, who founded the Albany Regency, an organization that dispensed over a thousand political jobs within New York State in exchange for votes. Van Buren then became Andrew Jackson's campaign manager, his second vice president, and eventually president himself. Incidentally, to engineer Van Buren's own candidacy for vice president, Andrew Jackson imposed a two-thirds-vote rule for all Democratic party nominations, a rule that was not eliminated until 1936.

Usually, at brokered conventions, where the bosses in "smoke-filled rooms" chose the party's ticket, the presidential candidate was not consulted about his choice of running mate. When William A. Wheeler was selected for the number-two spot on his ticket, Rutherford B. Hayes wrote to his wife, "I am ashamed to say, who is Wheeler?"[9] President William McKinley was not happy with the second vice president chosen for him in 1900, Governor Theodore Roosevelt of New York. The selection of Roosevelt is a classic illustration of boss control over nominations. Roosevelt turned out to be a wise choice, but at the time, his personal and political talents were not in the bosses' minds.

For boss Thomas Platt of New York, the vice presidency was a means of removing Roosevelt from New York politics. The popular governor was seeking to reform business corporations with which Platt's Republicans had profitable if not entirely ethical dealings. When Platt

Martin Van Buren's long and colorful career included service as a political boss and as New York State attorney general, United States senator, New York governor, secretary of state, vice president, and president.

offered the nomination to Roosevelt, the reluctant candidate complained, "I can see nothing whatever in the vice presidency for me. It would be an irksome, wearisome place."[10] Roosevelt only agreed to accept the nomination after he realized that without Platt's support he would not be reelected governor. He was also flattered to be considered for national office. Boss Mark Hanna of Ohio, the party chairman and manager of McKinley's reelection campaign, was gloomy about the prospect of an enthusiastic, unpredictable, energetic reformer as vice president, and commented, "Don't any of you realize there is only one life between this madman and the White House?"[11] Unlike previous vice presidential candidates, Roosevelt campaigned energetically across 21,209 miles, giving 673 speeches in 567 cities and towns in 24 states while President McKinley followed the presidential tradition of the times and stayed home.[12]

Other presidents also have been displeased with their running mates. Teddy Roosevelt was not enthusiastic when Old Guard Republican Charles W. Fairbanks was picked for his ticket. In 1920, Warren Harding wanted to run with Senator Irvine L. Lenroot of Wisconsin and got Calvin Coolidge instead. In turn, Calvin Coolidge was reluctant to have Charles G. Dawes as his running mate. For his unprecedented third term, presidential candidate Franklin D. Roosevelt was able to handpick his running mate, Henry A. Wallace, by threatening the convention that if he did not get his choice he would refuse to run again. However, when Roosevelt decided to try for a fourth term, a number of the party's political bosses plainly told the president that they did not find Wallace acceptable. Privately, they were aware of Roosevelt's failing health and expected that the next vice president would probably become president before Roosevelt's fourth term ended. They managed to nominate a reluctant Harry S. Truman for the second slot on the ticket with Roosevelt's blessing.

Traditionally, balancing a ticket for geographical factors has been uppermost in the minds of party bosses and the delegates they control when they pick vice presidential nominees. Arrangements are made to pair candidates who will appeal to separate regions of the country and bring in their votes. Before the days of instantaneous mass media, the party's two candidates could simultaneously make contradictory and inconsistent promises in different sections of the nation. In the earliest days of the republic, North-South partnerships developed, starting with President George Washington of Virginia and Vice President John Adams of Massachusetts, and including New Yorkers Aaron Burr and Daniel D. Tompkins, who served as vice presidents for Virginians Thomas Jefferson and James Monroe. As the nation expanded, East-West matches became more popular: Rutherford B. Hayes of Ohio paired with William A. Wheeler of New York; Grover Cleveland of New York with Adlai E. Stevenson of Illinois (grandfather of the 1952 Democratic presidential candidate), and for his second term, Thomas A. Hendricks of Indiana; William H. Taft of Ohio with James S. Sherman of New York; and Woodrow Wilson of New Jersey with Thomas R. Marshall of Indiana. The practice has persisted into modern times with John F. Kennedy of Massachusetts running with Lyndon B. Johnson of Texas, as an example.

Tickets were also balanced to unite different wings, or factions, of the party. In 1880, James A. Garfield, a Half-Breed (reform faction) Republican ran with Chester A. Arthur, a Stalwart (anti-reform faction), the protégé of boss Roscoe Conkling, who controlled New York State politics. The Half-Breeds wanted to reform the way government jobs were distributed and award them to those most qualified, while the Stalwarts preferred to keep party loyalty as the main criterion for government employment. In the

The John Kennedy–Lyndon Johnson candidacy of 1960 is an example of an effort to balance a ticket.

twentieth century, ticket balancing to promote party unity persisted with the nomination of conservative Charles Curtis in 1928 as a running mate for Herbert Hoover, who was seen as a liberal by many Republicans of that era. In 1932, the Democrats chose Texan John Nance Garner as a conservative counterbalance to their liberal presidential candidate, Franklin D. Roosevelt. The delegates' votes held by Garner, a presidential hopeful himself, were traded to Roosevelt to assure the Texan the second slot on the ticket.

Parties often split into factions because of disagreements about the crucial issues of the day. Presidential and vice presidential candidates are frequently selected to represent differing points of view—even though they need to work together if elected. In the 1840s, Whig party presidential choice William Henry

Harrison opposed slavery while his vice presidential partner, John Tyler, supported it. The Republican party's candidates in 1864, Abraham Lincoln and Andrew Johnson, were similarly divided on this issue. In the 1880s, Democratic nominee Cleveland wanted the nation's coinage to be based on gold, which would make it more difficult for farmers to pay off their loans or for businesses to expand, while vice presidential candidate Stevenson favored silver, which would have the opposite effect on the economy.

By the 1960s, brokered political party conventions had declined in importance, and primaries gave grassroots party members a chance to pick potential presidential nominees, sometimes committing party delegates to their choices. As a result, most presidential nominees select their own running mates, although they certainly consult with party leaders. (One exception occurred in 1956, when Democratic candidate Adlai E. Stevenson let the convention choose for him.) By making their own choices, presidential nominees could ensure that they had vice presidents who would benefit the ticket, who were politically compatible, and whom they could trust. Senator Walter Mondale filled all those criteria for presidential contender Governor Jimmy Carter.

Ticket balancing was not entirely neglected, but it included new elements. Previous political experience became a criterion for selection in the second half of the twentieth century. When presidential candidates campaigned as "outsiders," having held no national office, they chose vice presidential nominees who were more familiar with the Washington, D.C., scene. For example, the president who wished to remain "above politics," Dwight D. Eisenhower, ran with the rough-and-tumble campaigner Senator Richard M. Nixon of California; outsider Jimmy Carter, the Georgia governor, ran with Senator Walter Mondale of Minnesota;

and outsider Arkansas governor Bill Clinton ran with Senator Albert Gore of Tennessee.

Sometimes, however, presidential candidates choose their rivals for the nomination to be their running mates, a form of ticket balancing that can help unite the party or win blocs of votes from specific regions of the nation. However, this practice does not necessarily guarantee comfortable working relationships. President John F. Kennedy asked Senate Majority Leader Lyndon B. Johnson to join the Democratic ticket, not expecting him to relinquish his powerful legislative position. To Kennedy's surprise, Johnson signed on and broadened the party's appeal in Texas and the South.[13] Conservative candidate Ronald Reagan first tried to recruit the more moderate former Republican president Gerald Ford as his vice president, dangling before him the possibility of a more significant role than the traditional one of vice presidents. The idea attracted a lot of press attention and appealed to a number of Republican convention delegates. The presidential candidate, however, began to have second thoughts. He had been focusing on winning the election, not on the responsibility of leading the nation, and he soon realized that any relationship with his second in command that resembled a copresidency was not what he wanted. Ford graciously declined Reagan's offer to join the ticket. Reagan then settled on George Bush, despite the fact that Bush had condemned his economic policies during the primaries.[14]

Youth played a role in sixty-three-year-old George Bush's selection of forty-one-year-old Dan Quayle as his running mate. This type of ticket balancing had worked in 1816, when the Democrats chose forty-three-year-old Daniel D. Tompkins to run with fifty-eight-year-old presidential candidate James Monroe, after two preceding vice presidents had died in office. In the election of 1900, the Republican vice presiden-

*Dan Quayle was selected as George Bush's
running mate in part to appeal to younger voters.
Here, at a campaign stop, Marilyn and Dan Quayle
and George and Barbara Bush join a local parade.*

tial candidate, Theodore Roosevelt, was forty-two years
old, twelve years younger than his running mate
William McKinley. Aside from Quayle's appeal to conservatives, his youthful appearance and outlook was
expected to draw baby boomers and women into the
Republican camp. Bush, however, had done little
checking into the candidate's background, and
Quayle's political inexperience soon became a problem.

Despite warnings from the campaign staff, Quayle
compared himself to the young President John F.
Kennedy. Finally, he was challenged during a televised
debate with Democratic vice presidential candidate
Lloyd Bentsen. When Quayle claimed to have as much
experience as Kennedy had when he sought the presidency, Bentsen quickly retorted, "Jack Kennedy was a

friend of mine. Senator, you're no Jack Kennedy."[15] Quayle was also plagued by an unfortunate tendency to put his foot in his mouth when he gave speeches, and became an object of ridicule. Although the Republican ticket won, his verbal gaffes continued to keep reporters busy. One example comes from a speech in Nashville, Tennessee, when the vice president stumbled over the United Negro College Fund's well-known motto, "A Mind is a Terrible Thing to Waste," and twisted it into, "What a waste it is to lose one's mind—or not to have a mind."[16]

Choosing a vice president has presented certain problems for first-term presidential nominees. They often lack the time to consider a wide range of prospective candidates and to investigate their backgrounds for political or personal skeletons in their closets. In 1972, Democratic presidential candidate Senator George McGovern of South Dakota and his aides did not learn that their vice presidential choice, Senator Thomas F. Eagleton of Missouri, had been hospitalized for depression and treated with electric-shock therapy.[17] After he was nominated, Eagleton dropped this bomb himself at a press conference, having been warned that a newspaper chain was about to reveal the information. Members of the Democratic party were divided over the wisdom of keeping Eagleton on the ticket, since he had concealed his past until threatened with exposure and since questions about his mental health would draw attention away from the campaign issues. Although McGovern stood by his running mate at first, they agreed that Eagleton would withdraw from the ticket for the sake of party unity.

In 1976, Jimmy Carter was more fortunate. As a result of his primary victories, committing delegates to his candidacy, he knew he would be the Democratic standard bearer weeks before the convention met. He asked vice presidential hopefuls to complete detailed questionnaires and submit financial statements and then interviewed them. He selected Senator Walter F. Mondale of Minnesota.

Since ratification, or approval, of the Twenty-fifth Amendment to the Constitution in 1967, the president of the United States has been empowered to nominate a vice president, subject to congressional confirmation, if the office becomes vacant due to death, resignation, or succession to the presidency. Since the government was founded, the office of vice president had been vacant sixteen times for a total of thirty-seven and three-fourths years.[18] After the assassination of President John F. Kennedy, Congress finally decided to act on the matter. At that time, President Lyndon B. Johnson's health caused some concern, since he had suffered a heart attack while majority leader of the Senate. Moreover, his statutory successors, the presiding officers of Congress (the Speaker of the House of Representatives and the president pro tempore of the Senate) were elderly. A statement by Senator Birch Bayh of Indiana, chair of the Senate Subcommittee on Constitutional Amendments, explained why the replacement of the vice president had at long last become important.

> *The accelerated pace of international affairs, plus the overwhelming problems of modern military security, make it almost imperative that we change our system to provide for not only a President but a Vice President at all times.*
> *The modern concept of the Vice Presidency is that of a man "standing in the wings"—even if reluctantly—ready at all times to take the burden. He must know the job of the President. He must keep current on all national and international developments.* [19]

Section 2 of the Twenty-fifth Amendment to the Constitution was written to combine presidential selection with democratic choice. Ruled out were a special election by the people, which might be time-consuming and unsettling; a meeting of the electoral college, which had no machinery to investigate the backgrounds of possible candidates; election solely by Congress, which might be under the control of the opposition party; or selection by the president alone, which would not give the incoming vice president a wide popular base. The compromise of presidential nomination and congressional confirmation was acceptable to Congress and received the approval of three-fourths of the states by 1967. It would be put to use only seven years later.

In the fall of 1973, Richard M. Nixon's vice president, Spiro T. Agnew, faced charges of serious misconduct based on his actions while governor of Maryland (see Chapter 4). Under pressure from the White House and the press, and faced with the possibility of impeachment, he resigned from office October 10, having negotiated a plea bargain to admit guilt to a lesser crime. President Nixon was also in a difficult spot. He too was confronted with the possibility of impeachment because he had tried to obstruct government investigations into the 1972 break-in at Democratic National Headquarters at the Watergate complex. His outspoken and unpopular vice president had unwittingly been *his* insurance policy against impeachment, because members of the Democratic-controlled Congress were not eager to elevate to the presidency a man whose caustic comments had repeatedly been directed against them.[20] The resignation relieved the beleaguered president of a major problem. Nixon had not wanted his vice president impeached before he was himself indicted (charged by a grand jury with a crime), lest this set a precedent for the handling of his own difficulties.

Nominating a new vice president under Section 2 of the Twenty-fifth Amendment gave Nixon a chance to restore his credibility with the American public and Congress. The president preferred John Connally, former governor of Texas, but Connally had only recently become a Republican and had just been charged with illegal activities. Other choices were soon ruled out: Governor Ronald Reagan of California would alienate Republican liberals and moderates, while Governor Nelson Rockefeller of New York would antagonize the party's right wing. The most acceptable candidate was the twenty-five-year congressional veteran, Representative Gerald Ford of Michigan, possibly the only Republican the Democratic Congress would approve. Sixty-one-year-old Ford might serve as another insurance policy for Nixon, still facing the possibility of impeachment, because he was considered too much of a "lightweight" to serve as president.[21]

The FBI amassed seventeen hundred pages of information about the nominee after conducting interviews with more than a thousand persons. The results of the investigation were made available to the chair and selected members of the Senate and House committees who were conducting extensive hearings into Ford's fitness to be vice president.[22] After considerable discussion, the Senate approved him by a vote of 97–3, and two weeks later, on December 6, 1973, the House confirmed him by a vote of 387–35. He was sworn in as the fortieth vice president by Chief Justice Warren Burger before a joint meeting of Congress. After the simple ceremony, he told the assembled audience of dignitaries, "I am a Ford, not a Lincoln."[23] This plain, blunt, homespun man, the antithesis of a smooth, sophisticated politician, was soon caught in a dilemma: how to reconcile his belief in Nixon's innocence with the mounting evidence against the president.

Only eight months later, on August 9, 1974, Chief Justice Warren Burger administered the presidential oath to Gerald Ford in the East Room of the White

*Gerald Ford is sworn in as vice president
by Chief Justice Warren Burger as Betty Ford
and President Nixon look on.*

House. After consulting party leaders, lawyers, and members of his staff, Nixon had chosen to resign rather than endure protracted impeachment proceedings. As the nation's first and only unelected president, it was Ford's duty to nominate a vice president to fill the office he had just vacated, and he promised to submit a name to Congress within ten days. Among the front-runners were Republican party chairman George Bush and governor of New York Nelson Rockefeller. Rockefeller's knowledge of urban problems, corporations, and foreign affairs, as well as his proven administrative skills, made him the more attractive candidate. Although the sixty-six-year-old Rockefeller had often turned down suggestions to run for vice president, claiming he was not "built to be standby equipment,"[24] he changed his mind because "it was entirely a question of there being a constitutional crisis and a crisis of confidence on the part of the American people."[25] The Republican right wing did not balk at Ford's choice because it was considered unlikely that Ford or Rockefeller would run in the 1976 presidential election. On August 20, Ford officially nominated Rockefeller.

For Rockefeller's confirmation hearings, FBI agents questioned more than fourteen hundred people.[26] The disclosure of the nominee's gifts and loans to staff members of political colleagues, his enormous contributions to charity, and his substantial tax payments sparked debate over the relationship between political power and personal affluence, but Rockefeller was not seen as having corrupted politics. He was confirmed by the Senate on December 10, 1974, by a vote of 90–7 and in the House by a vote of 287–128 on December 19, 1974. On the same day, Chief Justice Burger administered the oath of office to Rockefeller in the Senate chamber, and in a brief speech the new vice president spoke of his "gratitude for the privilege of serving the country I love."[27]

Party politics and amendments to the Constitution have failed to produce outstanding running mates for the nation's presidential candidates. The most mediocre and venal vice presidents have been products of election by the House, the Senate, brokered conventions, and presidential preferences. No matter how the choices were made, no method satisfactorily screened out vice presidents who belonged in a rogues' gallery.

A Rogues' Gallery:
Vice Presidential Scandals and Follies

Conscious of my innocence, I feel outraged at the charges which have been made against me. . . .

Henry Wilson

NINE VICE PRESIDENTS HAVE BEEN ACCUSED OF MISCONDUCT, ranging from murder and treason to misappropriation of funds, alcoholism, immorality, and political corruption. It is tempting to blame the selection process for failing to screen out their character flaws and prior wrongdoing, but even if a screening mechanism had been devised, it would not necessarily have kept these individuals from being nominated and elected. Some, like Aaron Burr and Andrew Johnson, committed offenses only after they had become vice president. On the other hand, the offensive behavior of another, Richard M. Johnson, was known before he took office. Vice presidents like Schuyler Colfax and Henry Wilson, who served at the end of long careers, might have been thought more likely to have compromised themselves, but even Daniel Tompkins, a younger man just starting out in national politics, found himself accused of improprieties.

During the nineteenth century, vice presidential scandals might have been anticipated. The office held little power or prestige and failed to attract outstanding leaders. By the mid-twentieth century, however, the responsibilities and prestige of the office had grown, and the caliber of vice presidents had greatly improved. Nevertheless several officeholders, including Richard M. Nixon, Lyndon B. Johnson, and Spiro T. Agnew, were charged with questionable conduct their parties had failed to investigate prior to their nominations.

"We are indeed fallen on evil times. The high office of president is filled by an infidel, that of vice president by a murderer,"[1] lamented one senator in 1804. He was alluding to the fact that President Thomas Jefferson's vice president, Aaron Burr, had killed Federalist leader Alexander Hamilton in a duel on July 11, 1804. Burr was indicted for murder in New Jersey, where the fatal shot was fired, and in New York, where Hamilton was taken to die. (The vice president, whose grandfather, preacher Jonathan Edwards, and father were presidents of the College of New Jersey [now Princeton], had trained as a lawyer before pursuing a career in government.)

Burr was a longstanding rival of Hamilton, with whom he competed for control of New York politics. A few years earlier, Hamilton had circulated letters urging members of his party in the House of Representatives to vote against Burr in the tied presidential election of 1800 (see Chapter 3). As a result of his abortive bid for the presidency, Burr knew he would not be nominated for a second term as vice president and decided to run for governor in New York in 1804. When his party refused to nominate him, he entered the race as an independent and lost. For this he also blamed Hamilton. At a private dinner party during the gubernatorial campaign, Hamilton had remarked that Burr was "a dangerous man . . . who ought not be trusted."[2]

His comment was leaked to the press and published in the *Albany Register*. After Burr's opponents reprinted it in political circulars, he wrote Hamilton and demanded an apology for the insult. Hamilton declined on the grounds that such statements were to be expected in political campaigns. After further correspondence, Burr demanded satisfaction, and the two men finally agreed to settle their differences with pistols on the cliffs of Weehauken, New Jersey.

Although history has condemned Burr as a villain for shooting Hamilton, evidence suggests that Hamilton had intended to kill Burr first. Hamilton's dueling pistol was equipped with a hair trigger, designed to go off with the slightest pressure.[3] Burr, however, fired at once, hitting his mark, while Hamilton's pistol discharged into the air, scattering some leaves above Burr's head. After the duel, Burr returned home to New York but then fled to Philadelphia and beyond upon learning that he had been indicted for murdering his opponent. Some months later, he returned to Washington, D.C., a safe haven because it had no extradition agreements with New York or New Jersey. There, Burr presided over the Senate for the remainder of his term.

As soon as he left office, Burr and U.S. Army General James Wilkinson became involved in a shadowy scheme to invade Mexico with the possible intention of setting up an empire in the southwest. During the summer of 1806, groups of men assembled on Blennerhasset's Island, in the Ohio River, in Virginia, preparing for the adventure. Burr sent a coded message to Wilkinson vaguely outlining his plans, then headed to Kentucky to muster more recruits. In October, a nervous Wilkinson decided to turn informer and alerted President Jefferson to the plot. Two days after he received Wilkinson's warning, the president issued a proclamation asking public officials to arrest the conspirators. Burr abandoned an attempt to flee to New

An early engraving shows the historic duel between Alexander Hamilton and Aaron Burr.

Orleans and surrendered along with about a hundred men in December. From March 30 to August 31, 1807, the former vice president was tried for treason.[4] Finally, he was acquitted because two witnesses could not be found to testify in open court that they had actually seen him commit actions betraying his country, conditions required by the Constitution as proof of treason. Burr left for Europe and returned four years later, to spend the rest of his life in New York as a disgraced and debt-ridden man.

Vice President Daniel D. Tompkins had made a name for himself during the War of 1812 as a popular governor of New York, but his reputation was tarnished when he became the target of rival politicians who accused him of financial misconduct. Raised in Scarsdale, he graduated from Columbia College and went on to become a lawyer before entering politics. To help recruit and supply an army to fight the British, Governor Tompkins raised four million dollars; but because the banks refused to extend credit to the faltering federal government, he signed the loans himself and also contributed his own money to the cause. He did not, however, get receipts for his expenditures. At war's end, a grateful President James Madison offered him the post of secretary of state, but Tompkins turned him down. He hoped to use his wartime record and his successful governorship as a springboard to the presidency in the election of 1816, but the leaders of the Democratic-Republican party felt that the youthful leader lacked a national reputation. They nominated him instead as James Monroe's running mate, a welcome relief after the elderly vice presidents Clinton and Gerry, who had both died in office.

Once elected, the forty-two-year-old New Yorker spent much of his time in his home state, making arrangements to pay off bills he had run up during the war and in maintaining a lavish lifestyle. His friend, Representative John Taylor of New York, explained his absences from the capital, quoting him as saying that "there is nothing for him to do here, and any other man may preside in the Senate as well as he."[5] Loyal New Yorkers announced their intention to nominate him to serve again as governor in 1820 when he completed his term as vice president, but this would have thwarted the ambitions of Federalist party leader De Witt Clinton, the nephew of former vice president George Clinton. In 1817, after digging through Tompkins's records, Clinton and his supporters charged Tompkins with financial wrongdoing during the war because he could not account for a hundred twenty thousand of the four million dollars he had raised.

The vice president was guilty of faulty recordkeeping, commingling personal and government monies, and failing to get receipts for sums he spent on military equipment and supplies; but he had not deliberately defrauded the state. In April 1819, a state assembly committee under the leadership of future vice president and president Democratic-Republican Martin Van Buren, recommended that Tompkins's debt of $120,000 be canceled and that he be paid a bonus of $11,780.50 since he could have charged the state a commission on the money he had raised.[6] Tompkins argued that the state's figure was too low and that he was entitled to a 25 percent commission, instead of the 12 percent allowed him. The disgusted state assembly, controlled by Clinton, decided instead to sue for the missing funds. Tompkins's financial difficulties took a heavy personal toll, and he turned to alcohol for comfort and escape. His heavy drinking became a serious problem. One senator wrote that, "He was several times so drunk in the chair [of the Senate] that he could with difficulty put the questions [to a vote]."[7]

Publicity about his financial dealings cost Tompkins the gubernatorial election, but he was nevertheless reelected as vice president in the same year. He remained in New York, desperately trying to clear his name, so President Monroe sent him a special messenger with news of their victory. Tompkins was even sworn in in New York. Since he rarely traveled to Washington, in 1823 a president pro tempore was chosen from among the senators to preside in his stead. The effects of his drinking took a toll on his health. Yet in January 1824, Tompkins told Secretary of State John Quincy Adams that with the exception of sleepless nights, he had recovered; however, he was "determined to take no part in the approaching election, and wished for nothing hereafter but quiet and retirement."[8] He

Daniel Tompkins served two terms as vice president with James Monroe, but spent much of his energy fighting rumors of misappropriated funds.

died at the age of fifty-one, three years after leaving office. During his lifetime, the New York State legislature passed a bill to cancel the claim against him, while the United States Government declared that he was owed money as commissions for his wartime efforts. Long after his death, the New York lawmakers admitted to owing him ninety-two thousand dollars.[9] Tompkins was not completely forgotten; in 1827, Tompkins Square in New York City was named for him.

Senator Richard M. Johnson of Kentucky, whom Andrew Jackson had handpicked to be Martin Van Buren's vice president, was soon discredited because of his disregard for the social customs of his times. It was thought that the former Indian fighter, the self-proclaimed killer of the Shawnee chief Tecumseh, would add a rugged image to the ticket, offsetting Van Buren's reputation as a dandy. What the Democrats failed to consider was Johnson's personal life. He had lived for many years with a slave woman named Julia Chinn, whom he inherited from his father. She bore him two daughters, Adaline and Imogen, whom he proudly paraded before Washington society, offending the very proper citizens. Despite the social ostracism they endured as offspring of a mixed-race, common-law union, the daughters were eventually wed, both to white men, and their father provided well for them, giving them tracts of land as wedding gifts. After Julia Chinn died in 1833, Johnson took a series of black mistresses.

Johnson's personal life became an issue in the 1836 presidential campaign, the subject of vicious smears as well as charges that he intended to "amalgamate" the two races. The accusations took their toll, for Johnson failed to achieve the required majority of electoral votes to claim a victory and became the only vice president to be elected by the United States Senate, in accordance with provisions of the Twelfth Amendment (see Chapter 3). He did not spend much time in Washington, and in 1839 left the capital permanently to open a tavern and hotel on his farm in White Sulphur Spring, Kentucky. While discredited on the national scene, he remained a popular figure in state politics and was elected several times to the Kentucky legislature before he died in 1850.

Alcohol and politics are a poor mix and gave Vice President Andrew Johnson a bad start with the United States Senate. President Abraham Lincoln had quietly worked to have him nominated as his running mate in the election of 1864, which prompted Johnson to comment, "What will the aristocrats do with a rail-splitter [Lincoln] for President and a tailor for Vice President?"[10] A man of humble origins, Johnson had been illiterate until his wife taught him to read, and he had worked as a tailor to support his family before entering politics. When the Civil War broke out, Johnson had won Lincoln's respect for remaining in the Senate, representing Tennessee, while other southern senators had resigned, and he accepted Lincoln's appointment as military governor of Tennessee in 1862. As the nation's new vice president, Johnson was not eager to come to Washington to be sworn in. He was exhausted from typhoid fever and overwork, but Lincoln insisted that he attend the inauguration. On March 4, 1865, as Johnson waited in the office of outgoing vice president Hannibal Hamlin, preparing to take his oath and address the Senate, he had a few drinks to steady himself, and then a few drinks more. In his weakened condition, he was soon quite intoxicated. Nevertheless, he proceeded to the Senate and gave a rambling speech.

In a shaky voice, slurring his words, he recounted his rise from obscurity. "Deem me not vain or arrogant, yet I should be less than a man if under such circumstances I were not proud of being an American citizen, for today I who claims no high descent, who comes from the ranks of the people, stand, by the choice of a free constituency, in the second place of this government."[11] He went on to praise his home state of Tennessee, claiming that it had reformed and had abandoned slavery without waiting for Congress to demand demonstrations of loyalty. He also insisted that a delegation from Tennessee would soon return to Congress and that the nation's lawmakers would have no right to dismiss them. Lincoln was so embarrassed by the vice president's speech that he gave instructions, "Do not let Johnson speak outside."[12]

The Senate was incensed that Johnson would denigrate its powers and attempt to deny its right to determine the conditions that would allow the defeated southern states to reenter the Union. The lawmakers also found his inebriated condition most insulting to their dignity. The vice president soon had to preside over a debate to ban alcoholic beverages from the Senate chamber. Four days later, when the short session was over, Johnson left the capital to recuperate and never took up his Senate duties again. His relations with the legislators soon further deteriorated and resulted in impeachment charges (see Chapter 6).

Ulysses S. Grant's two vice presidents, Schuyler Colfax and Henry Wilson, were accused of corruption, two among many in the scandal-ridden administration of the personally honest but politically naive president. The 1868 election was the first time that running mates from neighboring states had entered a presidential race; Grant's home state was Illinois while Colfax came from Indiana. Colfax was a professional politician whose long career in the House of Representatives earned him the Speakership. (John N. Garner was the only other vice president to have served in that post.) Known as the Smiler, for his ready grin, he was a popular but not very distinguished leader. Colfax used his position as vice president to launch a bid for the presidency, which did not please Grant, who reversed his first decision and decided to seek a second term. Colfax then announced that he would be available for renomination as vice president in 1872, but Grant was so offended by Colfax's maneuvers that he replaced him with Henry Wilson, formerly known as Jeremiah J. Colbath. Wilson was a self-educated shoemaker who rose to become a prosperous businessman and a not very distinguished senator from Massachusetts.

In September 1872, the *New York Sun* carried banner headlines denouncing the Credit Mobilier scandal, in which Colfax and Wilson had been involved. Credit Mobilier seemed to be a railroad construction company distributing contracts to lay track for companies controlled by Union Pacific, its founder. Its sole purpose, however, was to get subsidies from the federal government for supposed construction costs and distribute these to the company's directors and shareholders as dividends. By overstating expenses, the company made a fortune in excess of twenty million dollars, which encouraged speculators to buy the stock, bidding up its price. As a result, Credit Mobilier's original shareholders could cash in their stocks and reap huge profits on their investment.

Among the original shareholders were Schuyler Colfax and Henry Wilson. To buy their silence and keep them from looking into the company's shady dealings, Credit Mobilier had Congressman Oakes Ames, an officer of the company, sell shares to members of Congress at rock-bottom prices. By 1873, however, public outrage forced the House of Representatives to begin an investigation of the company and the public officials who benefited from its operations. Colfax was the only lawmaker to maintain his innocence. He denied any involvement with the company even though Ames's meticulous notes indicated that Colfax was indeed a shareholder and had received hefty dividends. The lawmakers decided not to remove Colfax from office since his term was almost over. He spent the rest of his life on the lecture circuit and died of a heart attack in 1885.

The new vice president, Henry Wilson, initially denied the charges against him. "Conscious of my innocence, I feel outraged at the charges which have been made against me. . . . "[13] Then he explained that he had been given twenty shares of the stock but returned them without receiving any dividends and insisted that if any monies were paid him, he would return them. He also claimed that the stock was in his wife's name and had been bought for thirty-eight hundred dollars from contributions made in honor of their twenty-fifth wedding anniversary in 1865. A month later, he retracted the statement and admitted that he, not his wife, had purchased the stock. (She had died three years before the hearings were held.)[14] Congress cleared him, and he was not penalized for his part in the scandal. Wilson suffered a stroke shortly after he was sworn in, which may account for his lackluster performance as presiding officer of the Senate; he died in 1875, before completing his term as vice president.

Twentieth-century vice presidents were no more immune to scandal than their nineteenth-century counterparts. In 1952, Republican vice presidential candidate Senator Richard M. Nixon of California took to the campaign trail, as Dwight D. Eisenhower's hardhitting second, and ran into trouble over the funding of his travel expenses. Nixon, raised in Whittier, California, had worked his own way through college and law school. After service in the Navy during World War II, he entered politics, running for Congress and then for the Senate on a platform to rid the government of Communists. While Eisenhower remained loftily "above politics," vice presidential candidate Nixon repeatedly attacked the Democratic administration of Harry S. Truman for its laxness in ferreting out Communists in government, in pursuing the war in Korea, and in cleaning up government corruption. It was most ironic that in mid-September, while Nixon was accusing the Democrats of operating a "scandal-a-day administration," the *New York Post* ran a banner headline, "Secret Rich Men's Trust Fund Keeps Nixon in Style Far Beyond His Salary."[15] A group of California businesspeople had indeed contributed a total of sixteen thousand dollars in one hundred and five hundred dollar amounts to a fund to help defray the senator's travel costs as he crisscrossed the nation making anticommunist speeches. As a senator, Nixon earned twelve thousand dollars a year plus forty-five hundred dollars for expenses.[16]

Although Democratic candidate Adlai E. Stevenson had a similar fund, the press seized on the issue to strike out at the Republican anticorruption candidate, and even the *New York Herald Tribune*, a Republican newspaper, ran an editorial suggesting that Nixon withdraw from the ticket. In off-the-record comments, Eisenhower had told reporters that he did not know his running mate well and doubted that he was guilty of misconduct, but that nevertheless Nixon would have to convince the public that he was honest and ethical.[17] Nixon, still out on the road seeking votes and defending himself against the charges, learned of Eisenhower's remarks and was disappointed not to get stronger support from him. Republican leaders phoned the vice presidential nominee, urging him to go on television and explain himself to the public. If the nation accepted his story, he could remain on the ticket. The beleaguered candidate wanted Eisenhower, not the public, to make the decision after the broadcast, but he refused. Nixon interrupted his campaign and headed for Los Angeles to prepare his speech.

The Republican National Committee spent seventy-five thousand dollars to purchase air time. On September 23, 1952, just before he left for the studio, Nixon received a phone call from a Republican leader suggesting that he submit his resignation at the end of the broadcast. Nixon maintained that it was too late to change his speech. After only four hours' sleep, he was ready to begin his ordeal. Looking straight into the camera and speaking in sincere tones, he delivered a talk baring his personal and campaign expenditures. Nixon revealed that he drove a 1950 Oldsmobile, his wife wore a "good Republican cloth coat," and that the family had received the gift of a cocker spaniel puppy named Checkers. He claimed that since his daughters adored the puppy, "regardless of what they say about it, we're going to keep it."[18] Is it any wonder that Nixon's revelations have been known ever since as his "Checkers Speech?"

Vice presidential nominee Richard Nixon, in his "Checkers Speech" on national television

He also attacked the Democrats and Communists and anyone else who opposed the Republican ticket. "I am not a quitter,"[19] he told the viewing audience before urging them to let the Republican National Committee know how they felt about his remaining on the ticket. After vowing to continue his anticommunist, anticorruption crusade no matter what happened, he closed by reminding the audience to vote for Eisenhower, "He is a great man, and a vote for Eisenhower is a vote for what's good for America."[20] To Nixon's further disappointment, Eisenhower, while approving of his speech, would not discuss keeping Nixon on the ticket until the vice presidential candidate flew to meet him in West Virginia. After phone conversations among their aides, Nixon, assured of Eisenhower's blessing, left for the meeting. When his plane landed, Eisenhower embraced him, stating enthusiastically,"Dick, you're my boy."[21] Nixon put this scandal behind him, but there would be others (see Chapter 3).

Vice President Lyndon B. Johnson's questionable business dealings surfaced in October 1963 when his protégé, secretary of the Senate Robert G. "Bobby" Baker, was charged in a lawsuit with using his position to enrich himself. The son of a Texas state legislator, Johnson was trained as a teacher, but developed an early interest in politics. He entered the House of Representatives in 1937, before moving on to the Senate in 1948. In 1955, while majority leader of the Senate, Johnson had appointed Baker as secretary. He treated him as a son.[22] Baker was useful to the lawmakers, trading information, delivering campaign funds where needed, and doing personal favors. On the side, he had an interest in more than twenty corporations including insurance companies, motels, and vending-machine outfits. On October 7, Baker resigned his post under pressure.

The Senate Committee on Rules and Administration began looking into Baker's financial transactions, and the information the lawmakers uncovered proved embarrassing to the vice president. On November 22, 1963, the Senate committee heard testimony that in 1957 Bobby Baker had received a commission for securing a hundred thousand dollar life-insurance policy for Lyndon Johnson, whom most insurance companies would have rejected because of an earlier heart attack. In 1959, the head of the insurance company sent the Johnson family an expensive stereo set that Mrs. Johnson had personally selected, in gratitude for the purchase of the policy, and agreed to advertise on the Johnson-owned television station in Texas. In 1961 Johnson purchased a second hundred thousand dollar policy.

Vice President Johnson had feared that Attorney General Robert Kennedy, the president's brother, would prosecute the Baker case relentlessly and use it to keep him from running for a second term as vice president.[23] Despite Johnson's concern that he would be dropped from the ticket, the president heartily endorsed him at a press conference and the two men made plans to visit Texas in November. Whatever other motives prompted Kennedy to support Johnson, the president needed Texas votes to be reelected. On November 22, just as the damaging Senate revelations reached the press, an assassin's bullet made Lyndon Johnson president of the United States (see Chapter 6). The new president quickly distanced himself from Bobby Baker, even claiming that he hardly knew the man, and the issue was allowed to die. In 1967 Baker was found guilty and sent to prison for income-tax evasion and on other charges.

Elected for two terms as Richard M. Nixon's vice president, Spiro T. Agnew had managed to conceal his misdeeds. He accepted his first nomination with the statement, "I stand here with a deep sense of the improbability of this moment."[24] Agnew was the son of Greek immigrants who owned a restaurant in Maryland, where he grew up. Like Nixon, he had supported himself through college and law school. Republican Agnew quickly climbed the political ladder from Baltimore County executive to governor in a largely Democratic state. He was chosen to balance Nixon's presidential ticket in the hope of bringing southern voters into the Republican fold.

Agnew survived two national elections before it was discovered that his personal finances were not all that they seemed. Federal investigators had been tracking down claims that Maryland county officials received kickbacks for awarding public-works contracts to certain construction firms. In 1973, Lester Matz, Agnew's longtime friend and business associate, admitted, in a plea bargain, that he had been paying Agnew fees for giving government contracts to his engineering firm. The payments started when Agnew was county executive, continued while he was governor, and did not cease while he was vice president. Also, Jerome B. Wolff, a former Baltimore deputy chief engineer, confessed that the vice president had been paid some fifty thousand dollars in kickbacks by a Maryland construction company, Green Associates, Inc., and that some of the money had changed hands in the vice president's office.

The matter was brought to the attention of United States Attorney General Elliot Richardson, who met with the president and briefed him on the situation. Nixon, absorbed in his own Watergate cover-up problems, began to make plans to dump his vice president (see Chapter 3). He sent Richardson to Agnew, hoping to get the vice president to resign quietly, but instead Agnew denounced the contractors who had informed on him. Right after their meeting, the newspapers broke the story and Agnew issued a denial, claiming, "I have nothing to hide."[25] He repeated the same theme at a meeting with the president who seemed to agree with him, but then sent aides to urge the vice president to leave office.

Agnew decided to fight, blaming enemies in the Justice Department and the press for his predicament. As more stories about his misconduct appeared, however, Richardson decided he wanted Agnew out before the Watergate situation might make him president. President Nixon feared that if the vice president were tried in Congress, it would become even more likely that he would be next. Still resisting administration pressure to leave office, Agnew spoke to a conference of Republican women in Los Angeles at the end of September, proclaiming, "I will not resign if indicted."[26] The women waved banners inscribed "Spiro Is Our Hero!"[27]

In all likelihood, Agnew was holding out until an acceptable deal could be struck to protect him from going to jail. In early October, lawyers for the govern-

At an August 1973 news conference, Vice President Spiro Agnew denies any wrongdoing and insists he will not resign.

ment and Agnew's attorneys reached an agreement with Federal Judge Walter Hoffman that Agnew would not contest a charge of tax evasion; a fuller statement of the other charges against him would be placed into court records; he would pay a fine of ten thousand dollars; and then, he would be placed on three years' unsupervised probation. On October 10, after sending a letter of resignation to the president, he went to court. He left a free but disgraced man. In later years, Agnew went on to become an author and a business consultant.

One-fifth of the nation's vice presidents had their reputations tarnished by scandals. The various candidate-selection systems used had failed to detect flaws in their characters or past histories of questionable activities. Of course, no one could anticipate the misconduct that occurred while some vice presidents actually held office.

71

Politics Makes Strange Bedfellows:
Tensions Between Presidents
and Vice Presidents

I consider my office as constitutionally confined to legislative functions, and that I could not take any part whatever in executive consultations, even were it proposed.

Thomas Jefferson

ON MORE THAN ONE OCCASION, PRESIDENTS AND VICE PRESIDENTS have been sworn into office who could not work as a team. Their failure to cooperate was in part the outcome of vice presidential selection processes that did not consider political or personal compatibility as a criterion of nomination. Disagreements between these odd couples were exacerbated by constitutional responsibilities that gave the vice president dual loyalties, to the Senate and the presidency. A twentieth-century vice president, Gerald Ford, described the dilemma in these terms:

> *The Vice President is a Constitutional hybrid. Alone among federal officers he stands with one foot in the legislative branch and the other in the executive. The Vice President straddles the Constitutional chasm*

which circumscribes and checks all others. He belongs to both the President and to the Congress . . . yet he shares power with neither.

Historically, vice presidents perceived themselves as legislative rather than executive adjuncts and, until fairly recently, their offices were located in the Senate where the bulk of their nominal duties lay.

It is inevitable that a president's wishes will prevail, since a vice president has little power to dispense. Nevertheless, some vice presidents, like Charles G. Dawes, could and did embarrass their presidents by making inappropriate comments or speeches. On more than one occasion, vice presidents stretched their limited powers of presiding over the Senate to block the president's program. For example, Aaron Burr and George Clinton cast tie-breaking votes against their administrations, while John C. Calhoun named opposition-party appointees to committees. Others, including Thomas Jefferson, James S. Sherman, and John N. Garner, refused to carry out their presidents' requests. By these means, they undermined their presidents' policies, if not their authority. In turn, presidents isolated their running mates by refusing to solicit their advice, ignoring them, and turning instead to others for information and support—but they couldn't fire them. For better or worse, these odd couples were stuck with each other.

In 1796, the original electoral process outlined by the framers of the Constitution produced a Federalist victor, John Adams, and a Democratic-Republican runner-up, Thomas Jefferson. During the especially bitter campaign, Federalists had charged that Jefferson was a coward and an atheist and condemned him for approving the excesses of the French Revolution. Democratic-Republicans countered with accusations that Adams was a monarchist who schemed to have one of his sons inherit the presidency. Nevertheless, when the election results were in, Jefferson consulted with his fellow party member, House leader James Madison, to find out whether there might be a way to blend Adams's Federalist platform with the Democratic-Republicans' program. Madison thought the idea was impractical,[1] and the matter was dropped.

Just before the inauguration, Adams visited Jefferson and asked him whether he would serve as the president's personal representative to France to improve relations between the United States and the revolutionary government that had come to power. The two nations had been drifting toward an undeclared war, and since Jefferson was pro-French, Adams thought he could best negotiate the differences between them. Jefferson responded: "The Vice-President, in our Constitution, is too high a personage to be sent on diplomatic errands, even in the character of an ambassador. . . . The nation must hold itself very cheap, that can choose a man one day to hold its second office, and the next send him to Europe, to dance attendance at levees and drawing rooms. . . ."[2] As vice president, Adams himself had refused to participate in a 1794 mission to England for reasons similar to Jefferson's.

When Adams did ask him to sit in on meetings of the cabinet, Jefferson rejected the offer. The new vice president explained, "I consider my office as constitutionally confined to legislative functions, and that I could not take any part whatever in executive consultations, even were it proposed."[3] As a leader of the opposition, he had decided not to associate himself with the policies of the Federalist government. (No vice president would attend Cabinet meetings until Woodrow Wilson invited Thomas R. Marshall to do so.) Jefferson wrote of the vice presidency that "a more tranquil and unoffending station could not have been found for me nor one so analogous to the dispositions of my mind; it will give me philosophical evenings in the winter and rural days in the summer."[4]

Since Senate rules of procedure, still in the process of being formulated, were often ambiguous and contradictory, Jefferson spent his time as presiding officer of the Senate preparing a *Manual of Parliamentary Practice.* It was not adopted by the lawmakers but has been consulted ever since as an unofficial guide to Senate proceedings. In 1797, Jefferson wrote to future vice president Elbridge Gerry, "The second office of this government is honorable and easy. . . . "[5] It placed him in an ideal position to give his party the information it needed to discredit Federalist party policies in the next election. That wasn't too difficult to accomplish.

In 1798, the Adams administration passed the Alien and Sedition Acts, which made it a crime to write or publish attacks against the government of the United States. Scores of Democratic-Republican editors, authors, and speakers were arrested and convicted. Jefferson quietly spoke out against these laws and contributed money to editor James T. Callender, the author of vicious attacks on the president. When Callender was arrested, Jefferson defended him. More importantly, Jefferson drafted the "Kentucky Resolves," protesting the acts as an invasion of free speech and a violation of the Constitution. He called upon the states to denounce them and prevent them from being carried out. In 1801, when he became president, the acts were repealed and the imprisoned editors were pardoned. Jefferson had demonstrated that the duties of the president and the vice president could be conducted independently, with little or no cooperation between the two national officeholders of opposing parties.

Even membership in the same party was no guarantee of cooperation. Upon becoming president, Jefferson's relations with his own vice president, Aaron

Burr, were strained as a result of the tied election of 1800. Jefferson described Burr as a "crooked gun, or other perverted instrument, whose aim or shot you could never be sure of."[6] For most of his term in office, Burr was isolated and ignored by his party. He got even. In 1802, the vice president had to break a 15–15 tie on a Senate vote concerning a Democratic-Republican measure to repeal the Judiciary Act of 1801. The act had revamped the federal court system so that it could accommodate more judges from the Federalist party. Burr cast his tie-breaking vote with the Federalists, who moved to send the repeal bill back to committee, delaying its passage. To the Federalists' dismay, it passed the Senate a month later.

In 1804, Jefferson needed Burr's cooperation when the Senate, serving as a court, began to try impeachment cases to remove from office Federalist judges who had convicted Democratic-Republican editors under the Alien and Sedition Acts. As presiding officer of the Senate, Burr's rulings could help or hinder the administration's prosecution of the cases. Burr, himself a fugitive from justice (see Chapter 4), was able to take his place in the Senate because no state had jurisdiction within the District of Columbia. Thus he could not be extradited. In an attempt to win his loyalty, Jefferson arranged to have the New Jersey murder indictment against the vice president quashed, which also relieved the Senate of the embarrassment of having a presiding officer viewed as a felon. Burr's stepson received a judgeship in New Orleans, his brother-in-law was made secretary of the Louisiana Territory, and Jefferson even invited Burr to call on him at the White House.

The administration succeeded in ousting an insane federal district judge, John Pickering of New Hampshire, who was also a drunkard. Prosecutor John Randolph of Virginia, himself an unstable individual, botched the government's case against Supreme Court Justice Samuel Chase of Maryland. An ardent Federalist, Chase had been an outspoken foe of the Democratic-Republican party both on and off the bench, criticizing its members for promoting anarchy and atheism.[7] At the conclusion of the trials, one of Burr's most severe critics, Senator William Plumer of New Hampshire, commented, "Mr. Burr has certainly, on the whole, done himself, the Senate & the nation honor by the dignified manner in which he has presided over this high & numerous Court."[8]

No one was surprised that Jefferson had decided against having Burr as his running mate in the upcoming election. At the end of his term, the vice president retired from office after giving what is still regarded as one of the most moving farewell speeches ever presented to the Senate. Burr apologized for any offense he might have given to the members and urged them to follow the Senate rules of conduct that gave dignity to their debates.[9] As he left the chamber, he slammed the door shut behind him. By having had an important constitutional duty to perform, and having demonstrated his independence from the administration, Burr had gotten personal concessions from his president shortly before he left office, an example for later dissident vice presidents.

His successor, former New York governor George Clinton, was vice president during Thomas Jefferson's second term and James Madison's first term. The elderly vice president (he was sixty-five in 1804), complained about his duties as presiding officer of the Senate, "Sitting three hours in the chair at a time was extremely fatiguing."[10] Nevertheless, he wanted to become president and hoped the vice presidency would be a steppingstone for him as it was for John Adams and Thomas Jefferson. When the Democratic-Republican party did not back him

*An early engraving of George Clinton, who
served seven times as governor of New York State
and two terms as vice president, but failed to
fulfill his presidential ambitions*

and chose James Madison instead, he ran for president anyhow and was badly defeated. He was returned to office as vice president; an anomaly of the times let him contest both positions.

Clinton was so enraged by his defeat that he refused to attend Madison's inauguration and openly opposed his policies. He let the British ambassador know that he did not agree with Madison's plan to cut off trade with Britain. In 1811, he cast the deciding vote against legislation to renew the Bank of the United States, knowing how strongly Madison supported it. As a result, the United States had difficulty financing the War of 1812. Again a vice president had sought to undermine his president; but Clinton died in office before he could do more harm.

Like Clinton, John C. Calhoun was also a presidential hopeful who served as vice president during the administrations of two different presidents, John Quincy Adams and Andrew Jackson. A solemn, aristocratic, intellectual man without a sense of humor, Calhoun, a former secretary of war under President James Monroe, was a Democratic presidential candidate in the election of 1824. Crowded out by a field of four other candidates, he set his sights on the vice presidency and managed to convince competitors John Quincy Adams and Andrew Jackson that he would serve each as a running mate. The hotly contested election was thrown into the House of Representatives, as the Constitution required, because no one candidate had a majority of the electoral votes, although Jackson was ahead of Adams. With his own election secure, Calhoun played off both sides, promising them his support. When Adams was chosen as president, he rebuffed the vice president's attempt to nominate Cabinet members; but Calhoun did succeed in getting a postmaster general loyal to him. This enabled him to control the patronage (job distribution) of a number of lesser postal positions.

Calhoun, among others, felt that Adams had stolen the presidential election by agreeing to appoint Henry Clay secretary of state in exchange for his support. The vice president wrote that it was "the most dangerous stab which the liberty of this country has ever received."[11] Whether in fact such a deal was made is not known, but history records it as "the corrupt bargain." Although Calhoun admired Adams's intellect, he feared Clay's influence over the president, and worried that the Adams administration's positions on slavery, internal improvements, and tariffs (fees charged on imports) would be detrimental to southern planters whose interests he represented.

As the presiding officer of the Senate, Calhoun sat calmly while Senator John Randolph of Virginia bitterly denounced Adams for having made the "corrupt bargain" in speeches that sometimes lasted six hours. The president faulted Calhoun for not calling Randolph to order, but the vice president insisted, "I trust that it will never be the ambition of him who occupys [sic] this chair to enlarge its powers."[12] Adams and Calhoun took their quarrel to the public in a series of newspaper articles, condemning and defending the vice president's narrow interpretation of his powers. Adams wrote under the name of "Patrick Henry" while Calhoun took the pen name "Onslow," out of respect for a renowned British parliamentarian, Arthur Onslow. In fact, the Senate had long had a tradition of free speech and unlimited debate that the vice president could not overrule. It chose to resolve the dispute by giving the presiding officer the power to call senators to order for words spoken during debate, but gave the debaters the right to appeal to the full Senate.

Calhoun soon shifted his allegiance to the Jacksonians, who were preparing for the election of 1828. They had deliberately dropped the hint that their candidate was prepared to serve for one term only, to lure the ambitious vice president to their side. Calhoun further irritated his president by using his power to appoint Jacksonian supporters to Senate committees, where they delayed action on bills that Adams wanted. (From 1823 to 1846, when the congressional party leadership took over the task, the vice president had the power to name members to Senate committees.)

When Jackson won the election of 1828, relations between the new president and his vice president were amicable enough for Calhoun to get three of his supporters appointed to the Cabinet as the secretaries of the navy and treasury, and as postmaster general. Jackson and Calhoun, however, soon found themselves in conflict over the "Eaton affair" and the tariff issue. Cabinet wives, led by Floride Calhoun, repeatedly snubbed Peggy Eaton, wife of the secretary of war. In 1829, Peggy, the daughter of a tavern keeper, had married her lover, John H. Eaton, a protégé of Andrew Jackson. The wedding took place just months after her first husband, a naval officer, died at sea as a possible suicide. Jackson, whose late wife Rachel had been the victim of malicious gossip and social ostracism, refused to tolerate the Cabinet wives' conduct and called their husbands to task.

The wives stood firm, with Vice President and Mrs. Calhoun taking the lead by refusing to receive Peggy Eaton in their home or acknowledging her at social gatherings. Secretary of State Martin Van Buren, a widower like Jackson, took advantage of the situation to ingratiate himself with the president, whom he hoped to succeed, and gave a party in honor of the Eatons. The government ground to a halt as members of the Jackson administration supported one side or the other. In 1831, to solve the impasse, Van Buren submitted his resignation and persuaded Eaton to follow his lead. This led Jackson to demand resignations from the other heads of departments so he could reshuffle his Cabinet. During the reorganization, Calhoun's supporters lost their posts.

Perhaps the most bitter disagreement between the president and vice president erupted over the tariff issue. Calhoun had concluded that the 1828 "Tariff of Abominations" was detrimental to southern interests. For much of their livelihood, southern planters depended on sales of agricultural crops such as rice, tobacco, and cotton to European markets. Since the tariff raised the price of imported manufactured goods to discourage their sale, the Europeans could be expected to retaliate by not buying American produce, which would especially hurt southern planters.

In 1828 Calhoun had written *The South Carolina Exposition and Protest*, which held that states had the right to nullify, or cancel, any law that violated their interests. Calhoun justified this argument by claiming that the United States was a compact of states, not a union of the people. He claimed that the tariff of 1828 was unconstitutional because it taxed one section of the nation for the benefit of another, and should be nullified. As presiding officer of the Senate, however, the vice president could only sit by idly when Senators Daniel Webster of New Hampshire and Robert Hayne of South Carolina engaged in a debate over the doctrine of nullification in January 1830.

The president's position on nullification was first made known at the Jefferson Day dinner in April 1830, a gathering arranged to remind the Democratic party of its ties to Jeffersonian principles. At toasts given during the dinner, Andrew Jackson raised his glass and said, "Our Union, it must be preserved," to which Calhoun replied, "The Union, next to our liberty most dear. May we all

*John C. Calhoun of South Carolina played an
important role on the national political scene for forty
years but, like Vice President George Clinton,
failed to win the presidency.*

remember that it can only be preserved by respecting the rights of states and by distributing equally the benefits and the burdens of the Union."[13] The line had been drawn. In 1831, Calhoun became widely recognized as the author of the doctrine of nullification with the publication of his "Fort Hill Letter."

To widen the split between these two men, Van Buren arranged for Jackson to see a letter Calhoun had written in 1818, when he was President James Monroe's secretary of war. Calhoun had recommended that Jackson be disciplined for his overzealous and brutal conduct of the Seminole War. Calhoun defended himself to Jackson, insisting, "I never questioned your patriotism nor your motives," but Jackson rejected his explanations, stating, "I had a right to believe that you were my friend, and, until now never expected to have occasion to say of you . . . *Et Tu Brute.*"[14] The Latin reference—and you, Brutus—was to the words of the ancient Roman leader, Julius Caesar, upon being stabbed to death by his friend, Brutus.

As the election campaign of 1832 approached, Calhoun realized he had been duped, because Jackson decided to run for a second term. Since he was to be cast aside as a vice presidential candidate, Calhoun decided to get even with the man who had done the most to undermine him, Van Buren. After the Cabinet reshuffling of 1831, Jackson appointed Van Buren as minister to Britain while Congress was recessed. Van Buren had already been at his post for six months when the Senate took up the nomination, as required by the Constitution, and divided evenly on a vote to confirm his appointment. The vice president cast the tiebreaker and killed the nomination, gleefully announcing the results. Senator Thomas Hart Benton pointed out to Calhoun, "You may have broken a minister but you have elected a vice president."[15] As a result of Calhoun's action, Jacksonian senators pounced on him, attacking him verbally from the floor of the Senate. When John Forsyth of Georgia lashed out at him, Calhoun asked, "Does the Senator allude to me?" and heard the senator reply, "By what right does the Chair ask that question?"[16] As vice president, he was not permitted to participate in debates. Unable to reply to the attacks and with Van Buren soon to be designated as Jackson's running mate, Calhoun decided to accept South Carolina's bid to become a senator and resigned from the vice presidency on December 28, 1832. He was the first of two vice presidents to leave his post; the other was Spiro Agnew in 1973. During his disputes with the presidents he served, Calhoun had made himself a formidable opponent by using the powers of his office to the fullest.

Other vice presidents disagreed with the presidents they served and found ways to embarrass or to defy them. In the election of 1884, Democratic vice presidential candidate Thomas A. Hendricks publicly announced that his running mate, Grover Cleveland, should withdraw from the ticket after he was accused of having had an extramarital affair and fathering a son out of wedlock. Cleveland refused. Hendricks died nine months after he was sworn in.

Theodore Roosevelt's vice president, conservative Republican Charles W. Fairbanks, struggled with him for control of the Republican party. Opposed to Roosevelt's Square Deal, a series of reforms to help the middle class and consumers, Fairbanks tried to bury the measures in committee so they would never come to a vote. He also ruled speakers out of order on the slightest pretext, the most famous instance occurring in 1907 when his rulings killed a bill to make meat packers pay for the costs of inspecting their products,[17] a cause cherished by reformers because of extremely unsanitary conditions in the meat industry.

Roosevelt's hand-picked successor, President William Howard Taft, also had political disagreements with his conservative vice president, James S. Sherman, but they maintained cordial personal relations with Sherman serving as Taft's affable but inept golfing partner. During their first meeting at the White House, Taft asked Sherman to serve as a liaison with the conservative members of the House of Representatives. A former member of Congress known for his mastery of procedures, Sherman replied, "I am vice-president, and acting as a messenger boy is not part of my duties. . . ."[18] Actually, he did not want to turn against his cronies in the House and lobby for policies he did not personally support. Sherman tried, however, to counsel the president on the most effective ways to deal with Congress. The House was delaying action on a tariff-reduction law that would have fulfilled one of Taft's campaign promises. To get the bill moving through the legislative process, the vice president advised, "The appointing power is your only club,"[19] but Taft ignored this advice and found himself with the high Payne-Aldrich Tariff. Despite their differences, however, Sherman was chosen to run with Taft in the 1912 election. At that time, the Republican party, divided between supporters of Taft and Roosevelt, had paid little attention to the choice of a vice president. Sherman concealed that he had Bright's disease, a kidney disorder, and died during the campaign, too late for the party to pick a successor. Nevertheless, three and a half million Americans still voted for him.[20]

Disagreements quickly arose between President Calvin Coolidge and Charles G. Dawes, the only vice president to win a Nobel Peace Prize. (Dawes was honored in 1925 for finding a manageable way to have the defeated Germany compensate the victors of World War I for the damages caused by the German military machine.) Coolidge and Dawes were temperamentally unsuited. A man of few words, the president preferred to let events take their course, while his garrulous vice president was a man of action. Their difficulties began even before they were sworn in. Without giving Coolidge a chance to make him the offer, Dawes announced publicly that he would refuse a seat in the Cabinet. The vice president explained, "The Cabinet and those who sit with it always should do so at the discretion and inclination of the President."[21] Unlike other Cabinet members, a vice president could not be discharged by the president. No matter how accurate or self-serving Dawes's reasoning was, he could have discussed his views in private with Coolidge instead of taking away the president's initiative and airing his reasons before the press. Characteristically, Coolidge remained silent.

The inauguration gave Dawes another opportunity to steal the limelight from the president. After taking his oath of office, Dawes, who had never served as a legislator, lectured the Senate at length about the "filibuster rule." This rule guaranteed the right of unlimited free speech to every senator and was often used to defeat measures since any senator could talk a bill to death, or at least threaten to do so. Because lengthy filibusters kept the Senate from conducting its business, in March 1917, the members had adopted a cloture rule, allowing for the shutting off of debate and an end to the talking marathons, upon a two-thirds vote. Since this was difficult to achieve, the vice president challenged the Senate to make further reforms: "Who would dare oppose any changes in the rules necessary to insure that the business of the United States should always be conducted in the interests of the nation."[22] (The Senate dared "oppose any changes" until 1975 when the requirements were eased to allow a three-fifths vote to impose cloture.) The president's own inauguration speech was virtually ignored as reporters carried columns featuring, but rarely supporting, the vice president's remarks. During Dawes's

Charles G. Dawes, a person of energy and diverse interests, seemed to chafe at the restraints placed on a vice president.

term in office, the 1917 cloture rule was successfully used twice.

Less than a week after his inauguration speech, Dawes irritated the president again. The vice president usually took a nap every afternoon at his quarters in the New Willard Hotel. On the afternoon of March 10, he conferred with Senate leaders to find out whether a vote would be taken on Coolidge's unpopular nominee for attorney general, Charles B. Warren. Warren was criticized by Democrats and dissident Republicans for his ties to the sugar interests, an industry increasingly subject to government investigation and regulation. The vice president was told that six more senators intended to speak about Warren, so it was unlikely that a decision would be made that day. While Dawes napped, some of these senators changed their minds, allowing the nomination to come to a vote. Republican leaders realized that a tie was possible and sent for Dawes. When the vote split 40–40, they used every parliamentary tactic they knew to delay Senate proceedings until the vice president could return to the chamber. Jumping out of a taxi, Dawes scrambled up the steps of the Capitol, raced down the halls, and arrived in time to discover there was no longer a tie for him to break. One senator, Democrat Lee S. Overman of North Carolina, had switched his vote. The appointment failed to be confirmed by a vote of 41–39.[23] The president never commented publicly about this incident, but the episode made Dawes an object of ridicule in the Senate. The vice president was able to redeem himself as a presiding officer later in his term, and Coolidge actually relied on Dawes's late-blooming skills to ease passage of the Kellogg Briand Pact, outlawing war, through the Senate in 1929.

Dawes and Coolidge had another run-in, this time over agricultural policy. The vice president privately supported the 1927 McNary-Haugen bill, offering relief for farmers hurt by overseas competition, surplus crops, and lower prices. The president did not like the bill. Coolidge learned of Dawes's position when Senator James E. Watson of Indiana mentioned that the vice president favored the bill during a speech to the Senate, and reporters featured the story. Then the exasperated president allowed himself a rare comment about his vice president: "I have noticed that the McNary-Haugen people have their headquarters in his chambers."[24] When the bill passed, however, the president did not exercise his veto power to prevent it from becoming law. "A veto was action, and Coolidge hated to act."[25]

Although earthy Vice President John Nance Garner and patrician President Franklin D. Roosevelt worked well together during their first term in office, relations between the two men began to sour after they were reelected. Garner found himself frequently opposed to Roosevelt's policies. The president interpreted their 1936 landslide election as a mandate to press onward with his New Deal legislation to stimulate production, reform business practices, and offer relief to Americans devastated by the collapse of the American economy in the Great Depression. At Cabinet meetings, the more conservative vice president, a former representative from Texas, urged him to slow down: "Mr. President, you know you've got to let the cattle graze."[26]

In 1937, an automobile workers' strike led the two men to argue over labor policy at a White House meeting with congressional leaders. Garner, who believed that work stoppages were Communist-inspired, wanted the president to condemn sit-down strikes, where union workers occupied plants and would not let others in to do their jobs. Roosevelt refused to take his advice.

*N*ew York governor Franklin Roosevelt and Speaker
of the House John Nance Garner, newly selected
presidential and vice presidential candidates of the
Democratic party, make their first joint
appearance for the 1932 election campaign.

Garner admitted, "It was the hottest argument we ever had."[27] They also differed over deficit spending, which allowed the government to pay out more money than it took in as revenues from taxes and fees. Garner quipped, "I never heard of any other great nation trying to spend itself into prosperity by going into debt."[28]

Another serious disagreement between the president and vice president also occurred in 1937, when Roosevelt came up with a court-packing bill in an effort to circumvent the Supreme Court's tendency to rule much of his New Deal legislation unconstitutional. Roosevelt wanted to add extra justices to the Court, one for each judge over age seventy who had served at least ten years and refused to retire. Although the Democrats had an overwhelming majority in Congress, many lawmakers opposed this bill because the president's appointees might threaten the independence of the judiciary. Instead of using his influence to push the bill through Congress, Garner chose to take his wife to Texas for a vacation and rejected the president's pleas to return. His action led people to speculate that the president and vice president were quarreling, because Garner had never left Washington before while Congress was in session. By the time Garner came back to Washington, the court-packing scheme could no longer be salvaged, even if he had chosen to try. Then, when the president asked Garner for a blunt analysis of the situation, Garner said, "All right, you are beat. You haven't got the votes."[29]

Garner had returned to the capital to attend the funeral of his friend, Senate majority leader Joseph T. Robinson. Once more, he found himself opposing the president. Roosevelt and Garner had both agreed not to meddle in the competition to determine who would replace the popular Democratic politician; but then, much to Garner's dismay, the president pressured the senators into giving the post to Kentucky senator Alben W. Barkley. The vice president predicted that such high-handed tactics with the lawmakers would endanger the president's legislative program.[30]

Partisan politics widened the gulf between the two men. During the midterm elections of 1938, Garner did not support Roosevelt's efforts to purge the Democratic party of conservative senators who had opposed the court-packing bill. He dismissed the notion that the president could realign the parties into conservative and liberal camps and warned against the danger of what is now called the "cult of personality." "It's a risky business. When you build [a party] around a personality instead of a party program and principles, then your party is up Salt Creek when that personality is off the ticket."[31] Their final split occurred in 1940. After World War II broke out in Europe, Roosevelt made up his mind to run for an unprecedented third term. Garner, who had announced his own candidacy for president, vigorously opposed that decision as did Postmaster General James A. Farley and Secretary of State Cordell Hull. Garner insisted, "I would be against a third term on principle even if I approved every act of Roosevelt's."[32] Roosevelt was overwhelmingly renominated and went on to win reelection while Garner completed his term as vice president and retired to Texas.

When vice presidents and presidents were not politically or personally compatible, they failed to establish good working relationships. Vice presidents' dual constitutional loyalties to the legislative and executive branches of government did not encourage good relationships. In disputes with their presidents, they could use their formal powers, such as casting tiebreakers and recognizing senators, and their informal powers, such as giving speeches and writing tracts, to promote their own agendas at the expense of presidential policies. They could also refuse to carry out the president's wishes, but the president could not fire them. Because the vice president was the president's heir, their policy differences could have important consequences. The course of American history was redirected when some vice presidents who seriously disagreed with their presidents' views became presidents by succession.

Rising to the Occasion:
Succession to the Presidency

It is a mighty leap from the vice-presidency to the presidency when one is forced to make it without warning.

Harry S. Truman

NINE VICE PRESIDENTS HAVE BECOME PRESIDENT OF THE United States upon the death or resignation of their chief executives. The four nineteenth-century presidents by succession, John Tyler, Millard Fillmore, Andrew Johnson, and Chester A. Arthur, later retired to relative obscurity. Four of the five vice presidents sworn in during the twentieth century, Theodore Roosevelt, Calvin Coolidge, Harry S. Truman, and Lyndon B. Johnson, were subsequently elected president in their own right. Gerald Ford, however, was defeated. While most of these presidents dutifully carried out the policies of the presidents they replaced, three, John Tyler, Millard Fillmore, and Theodore Roosevelt, changed the direction of American history because they had not agreed with their presidents' views or they decided to use their newly acquired powers of office to carry out their own programs. Political compatibility with the presidential nominee had not been a consideration when they were picked to be vice presidential candidates.

In 1840, the Whig party chose an aging military hero, William Henry Harrison of Ohio, as their presidential candidate. For his running mate, they chose an experienced lawmaker and spokesperson for southern planters, John Tyler of Virginia, who was a recent convert from the Democratic party. The vice presidential candidate, unlike many in his adopted party, did not believe in strengthening further the prerogatives of the federal government at the expense of the states. The differences between Tyler and the party that nominated him became apparent upon the death of William Henry Harrison from pneumonia on April 4, 1841, exactly one month after the presidential swearing-in ceremonies. Vice President John Tyler not only altered political events, he also changed American constitutional history with the decisions he made upon taking office as president.

After a messenger arrived at Tyler's home in Williamsburg, Virginia, on April 5 with word of Harrison's death, Tyler decided that he would complete Harrison's term as president rather than assuming the role of an acting, or interim, president, as the Constitution's framers had intended.[1] The vice president returned to Washington the next day, having left the nation without a head of state for fifty-three hours, the longest period that the nation has ever been without a president.[2] He believed that his vice presidential oath qualified him to assume the office of president,[3] but to play it safe, he took the presidential oath. It was administered by Justice William Cranch, since Chief Justice Roger B. Taney could not be found. Under Tyler's direction, Cranch prepared and signed a document certifying that he had sworn in Tyler as president. Such precautions would be useful to the new president, for he soon faced a hostile Congress.

Before he died, President Harrison had called a special session of the legislature to meet on May 31. On June 1, the Senate received a message from the House proposing that a joint committee be appointed to inform the president that Congress was ready to get down to work and awaited direction from him. While Connecticut senator Jabez W. Huntington, a member of the Whig party, asked the Senate to accept the House proposal, Democratic Senator William Allen of Ohio did not think it was appropriate for Congress to address Tyler as the president of the United States and recommended that he be referred to as "the Vice President of the United States, on whom, by the death of the late President, the powers and duties of the office of President have devolved."[4]

Having set off a debate on Tyler's status, Allen allowed that the vice president would receive Harrison's salary for performing his presidential duties but should be regarded as an acting president. The Mississippi Democrat, Senator Robert J. Walker, insisted that the vice president inherited the office of president and not just his powers and duties.[5] Allen's measure was defeated 38–8 and the joint committee was appointed to meet with the president of the United States. That did not prevent Whig Representative John Quincy Adams of Massachusetts from referring to Tyler as "His Accidency."[6] Tyler's position was later confirmed by the Twentieth and Twenty-second Amendments to the Constitution.

The president's troubles with Congress had just begun. Senator Henry Clay of Kentucky, leader of the nationalist Whigs, was determined to enact into law his American System, a program designed to make the United States self-sufficient by integrating the industrial East, raw-material producing West, and agricultural South through construction of roads and canals. These Whigs had planned to use Harrison as a figurehead to promote their program, but now they were confronted with a new president who refused to be manipulated. To finance Clay's scheme, the party's members in Congress proposed a number of measures that Tyler found unacceptable, including a national bank and increased tariffs. In spite of Tyler's known opposition to a national bank, the lawmakers passed a bill establishing one. Tyler promptly vetoed the measure, but suggested that with some changes he might find it more acceptable. He went on to veto the modified law, claiming that it was unconstitutional because it did not sufficiently protect the rights of states.[7] In September 1841, some fifty Whig members of Congress retaliated by denouncing him and expelling him from their party. Since higher tariffs to underwrite the American system would hurt southern planters, Tyler vetoed bills to hike the rates. In January 1843, this provoked Congress to consider setting up a committee to investigate whether charges of impeachment should be brought against him. It failed by a vote of 83–127. Tyler was to use his veto ten times, the second highest total for the period.[8]

Tyler had problems with his Cabinet, too. The president had gotten off to a bad start with the heads of departments at their first meeting on April 6, 1841. Webster had asked the president if he intended to follow Harrison's methods. Tyler seemed to agree until he heard the secretary of state explain that all decisions in the Cabinet were made by a majority of the members, with the president having just one vote. Tyler then stood up and announced, "I can never consent to being dictated to as to what I shall or shall not do. I, as President, shall be responsible for my administration."[9] Responding to the bank vetoes, in September 1841 all the members of Tyler's Cabinet resigned, except for Secretary of State Daniel Webster, who was busy negotiating the Webster-Ashburton Treaty to settle a boundary dispute with Canada over the border of Maine and

New Brunswick. Before he left office, Tyler shattered a record for that time by having the highest rate of Cabinet turnovers, including five secretaries of war, five secretaries of the navy, four secretaries of the treasury, four secretaries of state, three attorneys general, and two postmasters general in just one term. Nevertheless, Tyler's administration succeeded in annexing Texas, reorganizing the navy, and initiating trade with China.

The Whigs' experience with Tyler did not keep them from making the same mistake in the election of 1850, when they nominated another aging military hero, Zachary Taylor from Louisiana, for president and New York lawyer and politician Millard Fillmore as their vice presidential candidate. Hoping to control the executive branch, Whig leaders had selected a politically inexperienced general who had never held public office or even voted in an election, while his running mate had not especially distinguished himself in the House of Representatives. The leaders may have thought that they had successfully straddled the issue of slavery since Taylor was a slaveowner and Fillmore objected to it, but they were in for a few surprises. The new president refused to be a puppet and struck out on his own path.

The burning issues of the day were the admission of California to the Union as a free state, and whether slavery should be extended beyond the borders of the South. In the Senate, such great debaters as Henry Clay, Daniel Webster, and John C. Calhoun aired their views in elegant and impassioned language; others resorted to name calling and invective. Unlike many of his predecessors, Vice President Fillmore had the courage to call unruly senators to order, but at one point, he could not prevent a hothead from drawing a pistol on a colleague. Henry Clay had already crafted a compromise package of bills to placate both North and South, but President Taylor, egged on by northern extremist Whigs in his Cabinet, stubbornly insisted that

California be admitted before the other matters were considered. Besides, he did not think it was appropriate for the federal government to make decisions about the issue of slavery. On the other hand, Fillmore supported the compromise, and early in July 1850 informed the president that if he were called upon to cast a tiebreaker, "I should feel it my duty to vote for it . . . because I deemed it for the best interests of the country."[10]

On the afternoon of July 4, Taylor attended patriotic ceremonies at the Washington Monument, where he consumed vast quantities of ice water, cherries, and iced milk to keep cool on the hot summer day. Predictably, he developed severe cramps, but unexpectedly, he also began to suffer the symptoms of cholera and typhus, two diseases that were sometimes fatal at that time. Having visited the ailing president on July 9, Fillmore was not surprised when a messenger appeared later that evening at his rooms in the Willard Hotel to inform him that Taylor had died. The new president was sworn in by Justice William Cranch at midday July 10 before a joint session of Congress and immediately let his views on the compromise package be known. Northern extremist members of Taylor's Cabinet, including the secretaries of state, the treasury, and the interior, immediately submitted their resignations, but the new president asked them to stay on for a month until he could get organized. Webster returned as Fillmore's secretary of state and, in consultation with Henry Clay, the new president appointed other nationalist Whigs to head government departments.

Between the ninth and twentieth of September, President Fillmore signed into law Henry Clay's famous Compromise of 1850, which admitted California to the Union as a free state, defined the borders of Texas, established the territories of New Mexico and Utah, and required the federal government to help return runaway slaves to their owners. The compromise averted

In an 1856 political cartoon dealing with the dispute over the extension of slavery, Millard Fillmore is shown (center) as the candidate of justice and moderation, attempting to make peace between the sectionalist candidates of the North, Charles Fremont (left), and the South, James Buchanan (right).

civil war for another ten years, but it took its toll on Fillmore. By signing the Fugitive Slave Law, he alienated most Northerners and divided the Whig party. Fillmore had written, "The man who can look upon a crisis without being willing to offer himself upon the altar of his country is not fit for public trust."[11] Ironically, the antislavery Fillmore accepted the odious provision that his slave-owning predecessor had held off accepting. His administration was credited with sending Commodore Perry's mission to Japan, which opened that Asian country to American trade. Unlike Tyler, Fillmore tried unsuccessfully to be elected in his own right as president, and was the candidate of the Know-Nothing party.

The selection of Andrew Johnson of Tennessee to serve as Abraham Lincoln's running mate in the election of 1864 was designed to balance the ticket of the Republican party, temporarily retitled the National Union party. The pairing of an Illinois lawyer with a Tennessee tailor did not, however, produce a president and vice president at cross-purposes. Both the Republican president and his Southern Democrat vice president were self-educated men who, as the Civil War drew to a close, adopted a conciliatory policy toward the states of the defeated Confederacy. Unfortunately, Johnson lacked Lincoln's statesmanship and political skills.

When John Wilkes Booth shot the president at Ford's Theater on April 14, 1865, George Atzerodt was supposed to murder the vice president in his rooms at the Kirkwood Hotel, but at the last minute he backed out of the plot. Unaware of his narrow escape, Johnson was half asleep when he was notified of the assassination and rushed to the dying president's bedside. The next morning he was sworn in by Chief Justice Salmon P. Chase at the Kirkwood Hotel with some senators and Cabinet members as witnesses. Johnson was determined to carry out Lincoln's plans for the South, which prompted him to issue a Proclamation of Pardon and Amnesty on May 29, in order to restore the South to the nation before the more punitive Congress reconvened in December. By then, six southern states were prepared to send delegations to Congress and had begun to enact "Black Codes" to deny former slaves political and civil rights and keep them impoverished.

An angry Congress led by the Radical Republicans, a faction eager to impose harsh reconstruction measures on the South, refused to admit delegations from the six states. In February 1866, the lawmakers passed a bill giving military protection to freed blacks who were denied their basic rights. Johnson vetoed the bill because it failed to provide for jury trials or abide by recognized rules of law. This action was upheld, but Congress overrode all of his other Reconstruction vetoes. Despite his appeals to the public for moderation, the midterm elections of 1866 produced majorities in Congress determined to impose martial law and military reconstruction on the South.

Scurrilous accusations that Johnson was somehow involved in the plot to assassinate Lincoln led Congress to investigate his private and public life, preparatory to impeachment proceedings. Failing to find evidence, lawmakers in December 1867 voted against proceedings by 57 to 108. They were given a second chance when Johnson decided to challenge the Tenure of Office Act of 1867, which required the president to seek Senate approval before dismissing government officials. Without consulting the Senate, Johnson fired Secretary of War Edwin M. Stanton, a Radical Republican sympathizer, and refused to obey the Senate's order to reinstate him. This was a bold but vital move. Had Johnson not taken this action, the presidency might have been held hostage to the legislature and never developed into the powerful twentieth-century institution it later became.

The House of Representatives quickly drew up and passed eleven articles of impeachment against the president by a vote of 126–47. Johnson's trial before the Senate got under way on March 30, 1868, with Chief Justice Salmon P. Chase presiding, as the Constitution required. Since the president declined to appear before the Senate, he was represented by a team of very capable lawyers who quickly pointed out the flaws in the charges against their client. The Radical Republicans, however, could not have cared less about the facts; their only concern was to remove Johnson from office. While the trial was in progress, Johnson commented

*P*resident Andrew Johnson *(left) consults with his counsel in his business office at the White House, to prepare his answer to the articles of impeachment.*

bitterly, "Bring me a list of the murderers of Charles I [king of England who was tried, convicted, and executed by Parliament in 1649]. I'd like to see how many of them came to an untimely end."[12] The proceedings lasted until May 26, 1868, when the president was acquitted by just one vote.[13] Johnson had paid a steep price for attempting to carry out his slain president's policies.

As the second vice president to succeed an assassinated president, Chester Alan Arthur seemed unlikely to pursue James A. Garfield's reformist policies. Known for his loyalty to Senator Roscoe Conkling's New York political machine, Arthur had occupied the lucrative post of customs collector for the Port of New York for seven years until he was forced out of office in 1878 by President Rutherford B. Hayes for padding the payroll with too many unqualified party members. As a

Stalwart, Arthur was nominated for vice president in 1880 to balance the ticket headed by Garfield, representing the Half-Breed, or reform, wing of the Republican party (see Chapter 3). Arthur claimed that "the office of the Vice-President is a greater honor than I ever dreamed of attaining."[14]

Vice President Arthur encouraged Garfield to appoint Conkling's supporters to government posts, but the president would offer the New York senator's people only some minor positions. Then, on March 22, 1881, Garfield ousted a Conkling appointee from Arthur's old job as customs collector and gave it to an outspoken Conkling critic, William H. Robertson, without consulting the New York senators as senatorial custom decreed. On April 14, Arthur pleaded with the president to reconsider his action, but Garfield stood fast. The vice president, siding with his former boss, Conkling, denounced the president to the press, "Garfield has not been square nor honorable, nor truthful with Conkling. It's a hard thing to say of a President of the United States, but it's only the truth."[15] Conkling resigned his seat in protest, expecting the state lawmakers to reelect him to office, along with New York's junior senator Thomas C. Platt. (Before the Seventeenth Amendment was added to the Constitution, state legislators, not the voters, chose senators.)

On July 2, while Arthur was in Albany, New York, attempting to get Conkling and Platt reelected, a deranged office seeker, Charles J. Guiteau, shot and critically wounded President Garfield at the Washington, D.C., train station. Witnesses heard him shout, "Now Arthur is President of the United States! I am a Stalwart of the Stalwarts!"[16] Upon hearing the news, the vice president returned to the nation's capital and met with Mrs. Garfield and the Cabinet at the White House. Embarrassed by Guiteau's statements, he returned to New York, keeping a low profile, and did not assume

*The assassination of President Garfield
at the railroad station in Washington, D.C.*

the duties of acting president during the eleven remaining weeks of Garfield's life (see Chapter 7). Arthur
was kept informed of developments by Secretary of
State James G. Blaine. At midnight, September 19,
Arthur learned that Garfield had died. At 2:25 A.M., New
York Supreme Court Judge John R. Brady officiated at
the swearing-in ceremonies with Arthur's friends and
son as witnesses.

President Chester Alan Arthur surprised many of
his critics by pushing through the Pendleton Act of
1883, which embodied Garfield's pledge to set up a
merit system for appointment to government jobs. He
also supported tariff reform, tax reform, and conservation of the national forests, and strengthened the navy.
While he included some Stalwarts in his Cabinet, he
gave the public an honest and effective administration.
Like the other nineteenth-century accidental presidents, he was not offered the chance to become an

elected president. The Half-Breeds could not forget his past ties to Conkling, and the Stalwarts could not forgive him for instituting reforms.

Thrust into the vice presidency to remove him from New York politics, Vice President Theodore Roosevelt unexpectedly became president. On September 6, 1901, President William McKinley was shot at the Pan American Exhibition in Buffalo, New York, by an anarchist, Leon Czolgosz. (An anarchist is one who rejects any government or authority.) Roosevelt rushed to the scene from a speaking tour in Vermont. He was joined by members of the Cabinet. Two days later, the doctors felt that the president was improving and that there was no need for the government officials to stay. Roosevelt left to join his family on a vacation in a remote area of the Adirondack Mountains, a move that helped calm the public. On September 13, he received word that the president was worse. After a ten-mile hike and a dangerous wagon ride down mountain roads, a special train brought him to Buffalo. On September 14, McKinley died. Federal District Court Judge John R. Hazel administered the presidential oath to Roosevelt at a private home before members of the Cabinet and some reporters. He was the youngest president to hold office. Having objected to his nomination as vice president, political boss Mark Hanna groaned, "Now look, that damned cowboy is President of the United States."[17]

Roosevelt announced that "it shall be my aim to continue, absolutely unbroken, the policy of President McKinley for the peace, prosperity, and the honor of our beloved country."[18] Returning to Washington, he held a formal Cabinet meeting and asked the heads of departments to stay on. In the three and a half years of the term he inherited, he embarked on an active program of domestic reforms that would have surprised the more hesitant and conservative McKinley. As he

*Theodore Roosevelt's enormous energy and forceful-
ness were an important part of his popular appeal.*

told reporters after he took the oath of office, "Due to the act of a madman, I am President and shall act in every word and deed precisely as if I and not McKinley had been the candidate for whom the electors had cast the vote for President."[19] As a forceful leader, he intervened to help coal miners during the strike of 1902, moved to regulate and break up corporations controlling American industries, promoted conservation of the nation's natural resources, and supported a number of domestic reforms. In foreign affairs, he enhanced American prestige abroad with the building of the Panama Canal and his insistence that the United States would become an international police officer monitoring affairs in Latin America. For his efforts, he became the first of the twentieth-century presidents by succession to be then elected for a full term of his own.

Former governor of Massachusetts Calvin Coolidge, chosen as Warren Harding's running mate by the delegates of the Republican convention, played a low-key role as vice president. He attended Cabinet meetings, but said little. He presided over the Senate diligently, but passively. When two members started a shouting match on the floor, he turned down suggestions that he rule them out of order, explaining, "I shall if they get excited."[20] On the Washington social circuit, the vice president lived up to his nickname, Silent Cal. One woman approached him, saying that she had bet that she could get him to say more than two words. Coolidge replied, "You lose."[21]

During the summer of 1923, President Harding decided to take a trip to the West Coast and Alaska to get away from rumors that his administration was riddled with corruption. Unknown to this carefree, poker-playing president, his secretary of the interior, Albert B. Fall, had taken bribes to lease naval oil deposits to private companies, setting off the notorious Teapot

Dome scandal. In addition, the head of the Veterans' Bureau had sold off government medical supplies for a profit, and other Harding cronies had helped people secure illegal supplies of alcohol after its sale was prohibited. During his trip, Harding sickened with a stomach malady and died on August 2 in San Francisco. The cause of his death has never been officially determined. Coolidge was asleep in his father's farmhouse in Vermont when a telegram arrived informing him of Harding's death. At 2:47 in the morning, his father, a notary public, swore him in by the light of a kerosene lamp. When asked years later about his feelings at that moment, Coolidge replied, "I thought I could swing it."[22]

Coolidge let events take their course. He was much more of a caretaker president than any of the other presidents by succession. Unlike Theodore Roosevelt, Coolidge believed that when a president died in office it was "the duty of his successor for the remainder of that term to maintain the counsellors [sic] and policies of the deceased President."[23] Given this attitude, he took no steps to disassociate himself from the discredited Harding government but simply stated to the press that he expected that the guilty would be punished.[24] Nor did he rush to demand the resignation of the two members of Harding's Cabinet who were accused of corruption and had not yet left office. Citing the Constitution, he resisted the Senate's demand that he fire Secretary of the Navy Edwin Denby, who was innocent of any wrongdoing. (Denby resigned voluntarily in 1924 to spare Coolidge embarrassment.) When Attorney General Harry Daugherty refused to cooperate with a Senate investigation, however, the president asked for and got his resignation.

The nation was prosperous and managing so well on its own that Coolidge felt justified in doing no more than four hours of work a day and taking long naps in

*C*alvin Coolidge, governor of Massachusetts, after his nomination as vice president of the United States

the afternoons. He summed up his philosophy of government with the statement: "If you see ten troubles coming down the road, you can be sure that nine will run into the ditch before they reach you and you have to battle with only one of them."[25] By not doing anything and not saying anything, he managed to get himself elected as president in 1924.

Hardworking Senator Harry S. Truman had been selected by the Democratic bosses and Franklin Roosevelt as the vice presidential candidate in 1944 because he had a solid reputation, came from the border state of Missouri, had a liberal voting record, and would not cost the president any votes. In 1944, the president's doctors realized that Roosevelt's health was poor but kept the information from him and his family. The president had a tacit understanding with his physician, Dr. Ross McIntyre, that he would not question his treatment nor would he be told what his condition was.[26] Democratic party bosses, aware that Roosevelt was ailing and probably would not complete his term, insisted that Truman replace the idealistic and politically naive Henry Wallace after Roosevelt's third term.

The Missourian was vice president for only eighty-two days and was poorly prepared to assume the presidency in the midst of World War II. After the inauguration, he had just two private conferences with Roosevelt. For much of February 1945, the president was absent from the capital, attending a meeting with British and Soviet leaders at Yalta. Before he left, he invited Truman to attend Cabinet meetings and asked the vice president for help in getting Senate approval of the nomination of former vice president Henry Wallace as secretary of commerce.

On April 12, 1945, Roosevelt died of a stroke at his vacation cottage in Warm Springs, Georgia. At five o'clock in the afternoon, his press secretary, Steve Early, summoned Truman to the White House where he was told the news. Within two hours, Chief Justice Harlan F. Stone administered the oath of office to Truman before his family and members of the Cabinet. The new president immediately asked the heads of departments to stay at their posts and, during the meeting that followed his swearing-in, told them he would listen to their advice, but that all decisions would be his to make and theirs to support.[27] Later he replaced them with his own appointees. At the conclusion of this meeting, Secretary of War Henry L. Stimson told Truman about a powerful new explosive weapon under development, but the president didn't learn that this device was an atomic bomb until his twelfth day in office.

At noon on April 13, Truman told a group of reporters, "Boys, if you ever pray, pray for me now. I don't know whether you fellows ever had a load of hay fall on

Vice President Harry Truman, with Bess Truman and their daughter Margaret looking on, takes the presidential oath of office after the death of Franklin Roosevelt.

you, but when they told me yesterday what had happened, I felt like the moon, the stars, and all the planets had fallen on me."[28] Truman faced a unique problem. Because the charming and forceful Roosevelt had served an unprecedented four terms in office, many Americans knew no other president. The new president had a lot to learn in a very short time, for Roosevelt had never briefed him on his policies, and as Truman wrote: "It is a mighty leap from the vice-presidency to the presidency when one is forced to make it without warning."[29]

Yet Truman managed a number of difficult and important situations, making decisions based on what he thought Roosevelt would have done and what he, Truman, thought was best for the country. Completing Roosevelt's term, the new president was able to bring

World War II to an end, using the atomic bomb against Japan. His postwar achievements included measures to strengthen the nation's defenses, to help Europe get back on its feet, and protect the free world as tensions mounted between the United States and the Soviet Union. He also offered Congress his Fair Deal, a program of social legislation reminiscent of Roosevelt's New Deal, that included universal medical care. The Republican Congress, however, rejected many of his domestic policies. In 1948, defying predictions of an overwhelming defeat, he won election to the presidency.

"The vice presidency doesn't mean anything. I'm 43 years old. . . . I'm not going to die in office,"[30] President John F. Kennedy told an aide, justifying the decision which made the powerful Senate majority leader from Texas, Lyndon B. Johnson, his vice president. (Ironically, Kennedy was suffering from Addison's disease, which is potentially fatal.) As his running mate, Johnson brought much-needed votes from the South, and would no longer be a rival for national attention in the Senate. Although Johnson felt that "power is where power goes,"[31] he soon found that he had all the trappings of office with little real responsibility. He chaired the Space Council and the President's Committee on Equal Employment Opportunity, traveled abroad as the president's representative, attended meetings of the Cabinet, and was a member of the National Security Council, which monitored international developments to protect the United States. His folksy manners and down-home speeches, contrasting sharply with Kennedy's sophisticated style and elegantly crafted phrases, led some of the president's assistants to privately call Johnson "Uncle Cornpone."[32] He had little interest in pushing the president's program through Congress after a run-in with the Senate when he tried to take charge of the Democratic party caucus and was rebuffed. Despite his trips and duties, Johnson was restless and dissatisfied because Kennedy excluded him from the inner circle of his advisors.

On November 22, 1963, Vice President and Mrs. Johnson were riding in the presidential motorcade in Dallas, past the Texas School Book Depository Building, when shots rang out, mortally wounding the president. Kennedy died shortly afterward at Parkland Memorial Hospital. Federal District Judge Sarah T. Hughes administered the oath of office to Lyndon Johnson on board Air Force One, which carried Kennedy's casket back to Washington, D.C. Among the witnesses to the ceremony were the slain president's widow, Jacqueline, and Johnson's wife, Ladybird. When the plane set down in the capital, Johnson spoke briefly to the nation, stating, "I will do my best. That is all I can do. I ask for your help—and God's."[33]

Half of the Kennedy Cabinet was flying to an economic conference in Tokyo when the news from Dallas reached them; the plane headed back to the United States. The heads of departments met with President Johnson and agreed to remain. Johnson explained, "I knew each of the men and I respected them. . . . I wanted all of them to stay."[34] Later, others replaced some of the Kennedy loyalists, such as Attorney General Robert F. Kennedy, John's brother, who had difficulty working with the new president. Johnson also set up a commission under the leadership of Chief Justice Earl Warren to investigate the Kennedy assassination.

The new president, formerly a commanding presence in the Senate, now applied his leadership skills to completing Kennedy's unfinished agenda. He told Congress that "no memorial oration or eulogy could more eloquently honor President Kennedy's memory than the earliest possible passage of the civil rights bill for which he fought so long."[35] Before the term was over he had outlined his own legislative program for the Great Society, involving a war on poverty, civil rights, con-

*L*yndon B. Johnson, flanked by Ladybird Johnson
and Jacqueline Kennedy, is sworn in as president
after the assassination of John F. Kennedy.

sumer protection, medical care for the elderly and the poor, and environmental concerns. He wasn't yet paying much attention to the war in Vietnam, but after his election to the presidency in 1964, his decision to increase American troops in Southeast Asia deflected attention from his social programs and cost him the support of much of the American public.

As the nation's first unelected vice president (see Chapter 3), Gerald Ford, a long-time member of Congress, extracted certain concessions from President Richard M. Nixon before joining his administration. Traditionally, vice presidents had borrowed staff members from other government agencies or depended on the President's staff to help them. In 1969, however, Nixon gave Spiro Agnew a vice presidential budget line within the executive budget, so he could have his own staff to write speeches, make appointments, and handle the press. Nixon agreed to let Ford increase the vice president's staff from seventeen to seventy and allowed him to hire and fire those who worked for him, a privilege his predecessors lacked. In this way, Ford made the office of vice president independent and self-contained.

The vice president spent most of his term in office demonstrating his loyalty to the man who appointed him. The president had told him he was innocent of any plot to cover up the break-in at Democratic National Headquarters in the Watergate complex, and Ford naively believed him.[36] In speeches all over the nation, Ford campaigned for Republican candidates in the upcoming 1974 midterm elections, praising the president's achievements and denying Nixon's involvement in the Watergate scandal. In view of the impeachment proceedings against Nixon, many expected the new vice president to distance himself from the president's problems, but Ford continued to defend Nixon without examining the mounting evidence against him.

117

On August 1, presidential aide Alexander Haig visited the vice president to tell him that in view of the latest evidence of the president's dishonesty, it was likely that Ford would soon become president. During Haig's recital of the options available to the incoming president, he mentioned the possibility of a pardon for Nixon. Ford refused to commit himself, a position the vice president maintained throughout the remainder of the crisis.[37] On August 8, Nixon summoned his vice president to the White House and told him he planned to resign from the presidency the next day. The vice president's transition team had already begun planning for a new Ford administration. On August 9, after Chief Justice Warren Burger performed the swearing-in ceremonies at 12:03 P.M. in the East Room of the White House, Ford told the American people: "I am acutely aware that you have not elected me as your President by your ballots. So I ask you to confirm me as your President with your prayers. . . . I believe that truth is the glue that holds government together. . . . That bond, though strained, is unbroken."[38]

Although he was the nation's first appointed president with no mandate from the public, Ford threw caution to the wind and started off his administration with two controversial decisions. He stirred the wrath of veterans by granting conditional clemency to draft evaders and deserters who had fled to Canada and other nations to avoid being sent to fight in Vietnam. Then, on September 8, he announced that he would grant an unconditional pardon to Richard Nixon. Although most other Watergate participants were already serving prison sentences, Ford justified his decision by saying that if Nixon were tried in a court of law "ugly passions would again be aroused. Our people would again be polarized in their opinions."[39] At first, the American public was outraged, suspecting that a deal had been made before Nixon left office. In all likelihood, the pardon did help heal the nation far more quickly than a trial would have done. While the public was still debating the pardon, Congress took up Ford's nomination of Nelson Rockefeller as vice president under the terms of the Twenty-fifth Amendment and approved the president's choice in December.[40]

Ford's verbal gaffes and tendency to stumble down airplane steps amused the viewers of television's "Saturday Night Live," which poked fun at his very human failings. The public was less tolerant of his inability to whip the economy into shape. In the remaining two years of his term, an economic downturn with high unemployment rates followed by rapidly rising prices did little to improve Ford's chance to win the upcoming 1976 presidential election. The desire to punish Republicans for the Watergate scandal did even more to contribute to his eventual defeat.

Vice presidents who became president due to the death, assassination, or resignation of their presidents were rarely outstanding statesmen or national leaders. Nevertheless, they provided stability for the nation, if not always continuity with their predecessor's policies. They also served as a constant reminder to the public that if a president is shot or becomes disabled, the vice president is just a heartbeat away.

A Heartbeat Away from the Presidency:
Vice Presidential Responses
to Presidential Disabilities

*The standing joke of the country is that the only busi-
ness of the vice-president is to ring the White House bell
every morning and ask what is the state of health of the
president.*

Thomas R. Marshall

IN THE PAST, WHEN PRESIDENTS BECAME ILL, THE NATURE of
the disability was often concealed from the public and
even from the vice president. This was the experience
of Vice President Adlai E. Stevenson, when President
Grover Cleveland was ailing. Although Vice President
Thomas R. Marshall knew President Woodrow Wilson
was ill, he had difficulty obtaining accurate information
about the president's condition. Often, during a president's illness, the work of the executive branch significantly slowed or came to a halt. Government officials,
such as Cabinet members, occasionally performed some
of the president's duties; but until President Eisenhower's illnesses, the vice president was rarely included
in this group. The Constitution offered no guidelines to
help those around an ailing president. They faced such
questions as how to define a presidential disability, who

120

should determine whether or not the president was unable to perform the duties of office, whether or not the vice president should become acting president while the president recuperated, and who should decide whether or when an ailing president could resume the responsibilities of office. The inherent difficulties of the situation could be further complicated when the vice president was elderly and ailing, like Elbridge Gerry, or held views significantly different from the president's announced positions, like Stevenson, or failed to develop an amicable working relationship with the president, like Arthur. Until 1967, when the Twenty-fifth Amendment was ratified, Congress debated the problem but failed to come up with any solution.

No one thought to make elderly Vice President Elbridge Gerry acting president, nor did he assume any of the president's duties when James Madison took to his bed in the White House, stricken with "bilious fever," in June 1813. Madison, nursed day and night by his wife, Dolley, had to lay aside his responsibilities for three weeks. At this time British warships were anchored in the Potomac River outside of Washington, D.C., as the War of 1812 dragged on. The president postponed a meeting with a Senate committee to discuss confirmation of Treasury Secretary Albert Gallatin as minister to Sweden and could not even read the batch of congressional resolutions Daniel Webster brought to him. While Madison was recuperating, Gerry came to call and decided that the president sounded almost like his old self but looked pale.[1] No attempt was made to hide the illness from the public, but newspapers fanned fears that the president might not recover. This prompted Congress to review the presidential-succession law in the event that both the president and vice president failed to complete their terms in office. By July 7, the president was well enough to handle the most pressing government business and afterward met with the Senate committee members who argued that Gallatin could not hold two posts simultaneously. It was soon business as usual.

Republican Vice President Chester A. Arthur showed no interest in taking over James A. Garfield's duties between July 2 and September 19, 1881, when President Garfield hovered between life and death with an assassin's bullet lodged in his back (see Chapter 6). Political differences divided them, and Arthur was in an awkward situation because Garfield's assassin had publicly announced that he wanted him to become president. Lest he be considered a usurper, the vice president refused to involve himself in government affairs and granted no interviews to the press. The shooting, however, was public knowledge.

After July 20, when the president's condition seemed temporarily to improve, a few members of the Cabinet were allowed to visit; but the doctors discouraged their patient from talking about government matters so that he could rest and recover. Garfield's only official act was to sign a government document on August 10. Members of the Cabinet tried to keep the government running and informed Arthur of changes in the president's condition, but there was much they could not do. Late in August, Secretary of State James G. Blaine circulated a memo on presidential disability and recommended that the vice president become president. Most Cabinet members were not eager to have this happen. They felt that in view of the precedent Tyler had set by refusing to become an acting president, Arthur would have no option except to complete Garfield's term, even if the president recovered.[2] Apparently, no one interpreting Article II, Section 1, paragraph 6 of the Constitution made a distinction between a vice president's actions when a president died and when a president was disabled since both situations were juxtaposed in the same paragraph. In any event, this vice president preferred to remain on the sidelines.

Following Garfield's death, the offices of both the vice president and the president pro tempore of the Senate, the third in the line of succession by a 1792 law, were vacant. Arthur summoned the Senate into special session to choose a new presiding officer. In his message to Congress, he asked the lawmakers to consider the problems of defining presidential disability and to develop procedures to keep the government operating, but no action was taken.[3] In 1882, it was discovered that Arthur himself had a serious kidney disease, but he chose to conceal it from the public and denied press reports of his illness. The next year he reduced his official schedule and did not begin work until noon. He lived to complete the remainder of Garfield's term.

In July 1893, Democratic Vice President Adlai E. Stevenson was not informed that President Grover Cleveland was undergoing an operation for cancer. The only government official told about the secret surgery was Secretary of War Daniel Lamont. All the public and members of the government knew was that Cleveland had gone on vacation and was cruising in Long Island Sound. Aboard the yacht *Oneida*, doctors anesthetized the president and removed a major part of his upper jaw. After a brief stay in his Massachusetts summer home, where he was fitted with an artificial jaw, Cleveland took a second cruise where more cancerous tissue was removed from his mouth. There were no visible scars to reveal what had happened. When a letter to a newspaper disclosed details of the surgery a month later, it was denounced as a hoax because the president looked and sounded so well. It wasn't until 1917, when one of Cleveland's doctors published an article about the operation, that the public found out what had happened.[4]

Vice President Stevenson was not told about the operations because he did not have a personal relationship with the president, and the two men differed over how to handle the nation's economic problems. The president went to elaborate lengths to conceal the operations because the economy was unstable. More than six hundred banks had failed, and it was feared that public knowledge of his surgery would set off a financial panic. Cleveland had already summoned a special session of Congress to meet in August to reduce the amount of money in circulation, a policy Stevenson opposed. Fortunately for him, the president was able to carry out his plans without the knowledge or the cooperation of his vice president.

When President William McKinley was shot in the stomach by an assassin on September 6, 1901, while attending the Pan-American Exposition in Buffalo, New York, Republican Vice President Theodore Roosevelt traveled to that city as soon as he was notified. McKinley was given ether while the doctors tended his wounds, but he soon regained consciousness. On September 13, he started to weaken from an infection, and the next day he died. During the last week of McKinley's life, no one pressed the vice president to take over his duties, and, in fact, Roosevelt left to join his family on vacation (see Chapter 6).

Democratic Vice President Thomas R. Marshall had to depend on newspapers for information about Woodrow Wilson's condition when the president fell ill in Pueblo, Colorado, on September 25, 1919. Wilson had been on a speaking tour to rally support for American membership in the League of Nations, the predecessor of the United Nations. He was brought back to Washington where his personal physician, Admiral Cary Grayson, announced that the ailing president needed to rest. On October 2, Wilson suffered a stroke that left one side of his body paralyzed. The public and government officials, however, were led to believe that the president had suf-

Vice President Thomas R. Marshall was a popular public figure, known for his humor. He was Woodrow Wilson's running mate in both the 1912 and 1916 elections.

fered a nervous breakdown with physical complications and that he was slowly recovering.

Before Wilson's collapse, Marshall had said of his job, "The standing joke of the country is that the only business of the vice-president is to ring the White House bell every morning and ask what is the state of health of the president."[5] The problem with the joke was that when Marshall did try to find out how Wilson was feeling, no one would tell him. Wilson had thought his vice president was a "small calibre man,"[6] which was probably one reason why Marshall was kept in the dark.

As early as October 3, Secretary of State Robert Lansing held a private meeting with Wilson's secretary, Joseph Tumulty, and urged that the president be certified as disabled so that the vice president could assume his duties. At that point Dr. Grayson entered the room, and both he and Tumulty swore that they would never issue the declaration. Then, on his own authority, Lansing summoned the Cabinet to a meeting for October 6, where Grayson told them the president had had a nervous breakdown. As Tumulty and Grayson were unwilling to attest to the president's disability, the vice president was not summoned to take over Wilson's duties. Instead, the heads of departments did their best to carry out the administration's programs.

On October 5, Vice President Marshall had asked Secretary of Agriculture David Houston for information about the president, but Houston professed to know as little as Marshall. That same day, Dr. Grayson spoke to Navy Secretary Josephus Daniels, who became the only Cabinet member fully aware of Wilson's true condition. Daniels urged Edith Wilson, the president's wife, and his doctors to tell the public the truth, but they refused, insisting that the president did not want to be pitied. Later, Mrs. Wilson asked neurologist Dr. Francis X. Dercum, one of the team of four doctors attending her husband, if the president ought to resign. He said that it would have a bad effect on the patient because getting the United States to join the League of Nations provided the president with an incentive to recover.[7]

When Wilson's wife and doctors finally decided that the vice president should be briefed on the president's illness, J. Fred Essary, a newspaper reporter, was asked to visit Marshall and give him the facts unofficially. Marshall wrote, "It was the first great shock of my life."[8] On October 11, an announcement was made that the president would be bedridden for "an extended period," and the pressure on Marshall to do something mounted.[9] He went to the White House to see the president, but Mrs. Wilson would not admit him to her husband's sickroom. As he told Arthur Krock of the *New York Times*, "I am not going to get myself entangled with Mrs. Wilson. No politician ever exposes himself to the hatred of a woman, particularly if she's the wife of the President of the United States."[10] He then decided that he would only take over if Congress, Mrs. Wilson, and the doctors asked him in writing to do so. They never did.

Marshall was reluctant to step into the vacuum created by the president's disability, although he was the first vice president to preside over Cabinet meetings. Wilson had asked him to assume this responsibility while the president went to Paris for the peace talks ending World War I. This time, he was not asked to act, so he did not. He told his wife, "I could throw this country into a civil war, but I won't."[11] To his secretary, Mark Thistlethwaite, he explained, "I am not going to seize the place and then have Wilson, recovered, come around and say, 'get off, you usurper.' "[12]

Instead of the vice president's becoming acting president, Secretary of State Robert Lansing supplied the leadership. Under his direction, the Cabinet met twenty-one times during Wilson's illness, but because the president was absent from the scene, much of the business of government had to be suspended. The League of Nations was defeated in the Senate in November 1919; many vacancies in government posts were not filled; twenty-eight bills became law without the president's signature; and foreign diplomats could not be accredited to the United States government.[13] Grayson advised that only urgent matters be brought to Wilson's attention. Documents and letters were given to Mrs. Wilson, who screened them and passed on the most important papers to the president. His responses were often illegible.

Leaving the governing to others, Marshall spent most of his time entertaining visiting dignitaries, such as the Prince of Wales and the King Albert and Queen Elizabeth of Belgium, on the president's behalf. He was not reimbursed for his expenses so he went back on the lecture circuit to augment his twelve-thousand-dollar yearly salary. Audiences enjoyed Marshall's witty, self-deprecating remarks. For example, he explained that the vice president is put "where he can do no harm. Among the other nameless, unremembered things given him to do is the making of him a regent of the Smithsonian Institution. There, if anywhere, he has an opportunity to compare his fossilized life with the fossils of all ages."[14] On November 23, 1919, Marshall had a bad scare while he was giving a speech in Atlanta, Georgia. The vice president was called to the phone and told that the president had died. He excused himself to the audience and rushed to his hotel, only to learn that the call was a hoax. Tragedy struck the Marshalls in February 1920 when the frail foster child they were raising suddenly died. They went to Arizona to recover from their grief.

As Marshall had predicted, Wilson grew suspicious of anyone who attempted to fill in for him during his illness. On February 12, 1920, the sickly and irritable president fired Lansing, branding him as disloyal because he had tried to keep the government running. In April 1920, the clearly weak president began to resume his duties and met with the Cabinet for the first time since he had become ill. Whether the decisions Mrs. Wilson and the president's doctors made were in the best interests of the nation, whether Marshall should have forced a constitutional issue, and whether Lansing should have acted as he did are still debated. Perhaps, had Marshall taken over as acting president, the United States would have become a member of the League of Nations because Marshall was more willing to compromise than Wilson, but this is pure speculation.

Unlike Marshall, Republican Vice President Richard M. Nixon was given the necessary information and the opportunity to provide leadership during President Dwight D. Eisenhower's three illnesses. He was

*P*atricia and Richard M. Nixon and Dwight and
Mamie Eisenhower enjoy an ovation from the crowd
at the 1952 Republican Convention.

the first vice president to serve as an effective if unofficial caretaker for an ailing president. Congress, however,
had still not taken steps to clarify the constitutional provisions concerning presidential disabilities. In that
respect, Nixon's position was not so different from
Marshall's; but this time, the government did not come
to a standstill. Eisenhower more readily delegated responsibility to others than did Wilson, so when he became sick, members of his administration were accustomed to functioning as a team.

Nixon read a newspaper article that the president
had suffered a bout of indigestion on September 24,
1955, in Denver, Colorado, where he had been vaca-
tioning. The vice president thought nothing of it until
the president's press secretary, James Hagerty, phoned

to tell him that Eisenhower had actually suffered a moderate heart attack. A false story had been planted in the newspapers to avoid upsetting the nation. When an accurate account of the president's condition was released, Nixon avoided photographers milling outside his home because he knew that whether he smiled or frowned his image could easily be misinterpreted by the public. He chose to be cautious for he had been criticized in the media for his youth, and extremely partisan attacks on the Democrats, and doubts had been expressed about his ability to serve as president. Later he wrote about his dilemma:

> *Certainly I had no desire or intention to seize an iota of presidential power. I was the vice president and could be nothing more. But the problem was to guard against what I knew would be easy misinterpretation of any mistake, no matter how slight, I might make in public or private. . . . My problem, what I had to do, was to provide leadership without appearing to lead.*[15]

Eisenhower, mindful of the problems caused by secrecy about Wilson's illness, issued orders from his hospital bed that the state of his health be made public and that the National Security Council (NSC) and the Cabinet meet under the direction of the vice president. The next day, Nixon assured the nation that the president's policies would be carried out. He signed some nonlegal papers in the president's name and met with the NSC and the Cabinet. At the Cabinet meeting, it was decided that heads of departments would handle routine matters on their own, as they usually did; that questions normally discussed at Cabinet meetings would be taken up there; and that decisions requiring the president's attention would first be discussed in the Cabinet and by the NSC before being sent to Eisenhower in Denver.[16] To make certain that he was perceived as vice president and not as acting president,

Nixon sat in his regular seat during these meetings and conducted business from his own office.

Over Nixon's objections, Secretary of State John Foster Dulles and presidential chief of staff Sherman Adams got the Cabinet and the NSC to agree to let Adams serve as liaison to Eisenhower, flying to Denver to brief him on Cabinet meetings and other matters, and getting his signature where needed. Nixon had wanted Adams to run things from the White House, and thus keep the action in Washington, Nixon's own base of operations.[17] However, he was overruled by Dulles. The secretary of state remembered the penalty his uncle, Robert Lansing, had paid for holding Cabinet meetings while Wilson was ill[18] and insisted that Adams shuttle back and forth from Denver to Washington to keep the president informed. It is also possible that he, the chief of staff, and the president did not completely trust the vice president and feared Nixon would use the president's illness to advance his own political career. Eisenhower reinforced Dulles's position by writing to Nixon that he wanted Dulles to handle things in Washington.

The center of power effectively shifted from the capital to Colorado, reducing Nixon's prominence as a caretaker. In this way, Eisenhower left himself room to maneuver if he decided to drop the controversial vice president from the ticket in the upcoming 1956 elections.[19] Nixon visited the president in Denver on October 8, a week after Adams began his "messenger service," and then continued to preside over Cabinet and NSC meetings while "Adams ran the government."[20] Nixon called the arrangement "the committee system," and felt it worked well because no major international crisis erupted.[21] At this time, tensions with the Soviet Union and problems in the Mideast often dominated the headlines.

The president's other two illnesses were even less demanding for the vice president. On June 7, 1956,

Eisenhower was stricken with ileitis, inflammation of the small intestine, and underwent surgery at Walter Reed Hospital the next day to relieve the condition. He was under anesthesia for two hours, but no emergency government procedures were instituted. The president quickly recovered and was able to perform his official duties a few days later.

The public, informed of developments, had enough confidence in the Eisenhower team to give them a second term in the 1956 elections. Then, on November 25, 1957, just as Americans learned that the Soviet Union had launched Sputnik, the world's first artificial satellite, the president suffered a moderate stroke, initially affecting his speech. Eisenhower confided to Adams that if he could not perform his duties, he would give up the presidency. Adams told Nixon, "You may be President in the next twenty-four hours,"[22] but the president quickly improved and was back at work by December 2.

In 1956 and again in 1957, Eisenhower tried to get Congress to propose a constitutional amendment to cover situations where the president was unable to declare his own disability. The Department of Justice had looked into the matter and its findings were reviewed at a Cabinet meeting. Eisenhower favored the creation of a commission made up of the chief justice and doctors to declare the president incapacitated, while the attorney general preferred having the vice president and the Cabinet certify the president's disability. The latter position was endorsed by the Cabinet and presented to congressional leaders in 1957. The Republican lawmakers objected that Congress would not be consulted, and the Democrats opposed any attempt by the president to turn his duties over to someone else, especially Richard Nixon, a prospective candidate in the 1960 election.

With Congress unwilling to act, Eisenhower and Nixon signed an informal agreement providing that the president would inform the vice president if he were unable to perform his duties. If the president could not communicate, the vice president would decide, after such consultation as he chose to make, whether the president was incapacitated. In the event of a disability, the vice president would serve as acting president. The president would decide if and when he was prepared to resume his responsibilities. The letter was made public March 3, 1958. Similar arrangements were adopted between President Kennedy and Vice President Johnson and between President Johnson and Vice President Humphrey.[23]

The Twenty-fifth Amendment was designed to clarify and formalize these private agreements and to outline a procedure for filling vice presidential vacancies. Democratic Senator Birch Bayh, chairman of the Subcommittee on Constitutional Amendments, began hearings in 1964 to resolve the issue of presidential succession and disability. As he explained:

> *Here we have a constitutional gap, a blind spot, if you will. We must fill this gap if we are to protect our Nation from the possibility of floundering in the sea of public confusion and uncertainty which ofttimes exists at times of national peril and tragedy.*[24]

Section 1 of the amendment makes clear that upon the death, resignation, or removal of a president, the vice president becomes president, not acting president, while Section 2 focuses on selecting replacement vice presidents.

Sections 3 and 4 outline an elaborate process for handling presidential disabilities. In effect, the president or the vice president, together with a majority of the

Cabinet, inform Congress that a disability exists. Then the vice president functions as acting president. When the president declares that he is no longer disabled, he resumes his duties unless the vice president and a majority of the Cabinet disagree. In that event, Congress must resolve the issue within twenty-one days. Under these circumstances, a two-thirds vote in both houses is needed to remove the president. If the Cabinet is unable to reach a decision, Congress can designate another body to make the decision with the vice president.[25]

On March 30, 1981, Vice President George Bush was flying from Fort Worth to Austin, Texas, to address the state legislature when John W. Hinckley Jr. shot President Ronald W. Reagan outside the Washington Hilton Hotel, piercing his left lung. The seventy-year-old president was rushed to George Washington University Hospital where his wife, Nancy, joined him, while Bush headed back to the nation's capital. Members of the president's Cabinet and White House staff met in the Situation Room of the White House with not much more information than had been made public. They had been in office for only seventy days and had not yet developed guidelines for handling a presidential disability. When Deputy Press Secretary Larry Speakes became flustered and could not answer a number of the reporters' questions, Secretary of State Alexander Haig dashed to the pressroom and in response to the question, "who is making the decisions for the government right now?" said, "Constitutionally, gentlemen, you have the president, the vice president, and the secretary of state, in that order. . . . As of now, I am in control here. . . ."[26] His words might have had a more calming effect on the public if he had taken the time to catch his breath, wipe the perspiration from his brow, and check his facts before he appeared on television. The Speaker of the House of Representatives is third in the line of presidential succession.

Vice President George Bush, with secret service agents and staff, leaves the White House to visit President Reagan in the hospital after the 1981 attempt on the president's life.

That afternoon, after learning that the president was stable and that the prospects for his recovery were good, Reagan administration officials decided not to invoke the Twenty-fifth Amendment, transferring power to George Bush. White House deputy chief of staff Richard Darman locked the transfer papers in a White House safe. The decision was made by an informal group without convening the Cabinet or consulting with the vice president as the amendment required. They felt that if Bush had become acting president, the American people and the nation's allies would have concluded that Reagan was more seriously wounded than he seemed to be.[27]

To avoid alarming the public, when the vice president returned to Washington, D.C., he went to his own residence and then drove over to the White House, rather than flying there directly by helicopter.[28] Presidential aides reviewed the disability clauses of the Twenty-fifth amendment with him; but, like Thomas Marshall before him, Bush was wary of any move that might be misinterpreted as usurping presidential power. On March 31, he performed ceremonial duties and met with the Cabinet, but like Nixon, he did not occupy the Oval Office or the president's chair in the Cabinet Room. The administration gave the public the impression that Reagan was governing soon after the shooting, but this was not true. Vice President Bush presided over Cabinet meetings for almost a month, and the president did not work a full day until June 3. Unlike the Eisenhower team, which was candid with the American people, the Reagan administration, preoccupied with the president's image, was more willing to mislead the public, recalling the handling of Wilson's illness.

On July 12, 1985, President Reagan was admitted to Bethesda Naval Hospital for removal of a noncancerous growth. The night before the surgery, Bush remained at his home in Maine to minimize public concern and flew back to the capital the next day. Before the president was anesthetized, he signed a document which was sent to Congress, transferring power to the vice president. He made George Bush acting president without formally invoking Section 3 of the Twenty-fifth Amendment. While Reagan had followed the procedures outlined in the amendment, he insisted that since his was a temporary period of disability, "I do not believe that the drafters of this Amendment intended its application to situations such as the instant one."[29] For eight hours, Acting President Bush simply stayed home and waited for Reagan to recover consciousness.

When the president awakened, White House counsel Fred Fielding and chief of staff Donald Regan handed him a two-sentence letter to test whether he was ready to take charge again. The letter concerned his resumption of presidential duties, and once he had read it, Reagan immediately said, "Gimme a pen,"[30] and signed it. In doing so, he followed the guidelines established by the Twenty-fifth Amendment once more. In their memoirs, both Ronald and Nancy Reagan claimed that the Twenty-fifth Amendment had been used, a position supported by Fielding and Regan.[31] Yet Reagan had deliberately denied that he was invoking the amendment while he held office, lest the nation and the world think he was disabled. Once more, concern over his image had affected Reagan's decisions; as the nation's oldest president, he did not want to appear to have lost his vigor or vitality. On July 22, the president left the hospital and by the beginning of September was back to a full schedule of work.

On April 28, 1989, President George Bush's press secretary, Marlin Fitzwater, told reporters at a briefing session that the president, his wife Barbara, Vice President Dan Quayle, chief of staff John Sununu and others had met to discuss procedures required by the Twenty-fifth Amendment, to make sure that everyone was familiar with them. The meeting was a response to recommendations of the 1988 Miller Commission, a panel of political, legal, and medical experts who met to study how the Twenty-fifth Amendment had been used. The commission made a number of recommendations to help the White House better prepare for presidential disabilities. Among the suggestions were increasing the role of the White House physician to monitor the president's health; developing separate written guidelines for a health emergency, a planned operation, and a chronic illness; and making the amendment a regular process of government, familiar to the public.[32] Letters naming Vice President Quayle as acting president were prepared but never used. On May 4, 1991, George Bush was hospitalized for an irregular heartbeat, but he was not given an anesthetic and returned to the White House two days later. On a trip to Japan eight months later, he took sick with an intestinal virus but recovered the next day.

The Twenty-fifth Amendment has provided procedures to give the vice president a greater role in deciding presidential disabilities and running the government so that the administration will not come to a standstill when a president is incapacitated. Now the vice president has guidelines and thus does not have to stay on the sidelines for fear of being accused of usurping power when a president is not up to the duties of the office. It is an important step in the direction of making vice presidents team players within presidential administrations.

• C H A P T E R   E I G H T •

Being a Team Player:
The Expansion of
Vice Presidential Duties

My principal goal is to help the President do the best he possibly can, and so my own record as Vice-President is necessarily obscured, in significant measure because so much of my energy goes into trying to help him.

Albert Gore

VICE PRESIDENTS WHO WERE POLITICALLY AND PERSONALLY compatible with their running mates often became team players. If, like Mondale or Bush, they disagreed with a presidential program, they voiced their objections privately. Following the example of George M. Dallas and Garret A. Hobart, they performed their constitutional duties of presiding over the Senate and casting tiebreakers to support their presidents' policies. Having proved themselves trustworthy members of the administration, some vice presidents, including John Nance Garner, Henry A. Wallace, and Alben W. Barkley, were given additional political, policy, and ceremonial duties to perform. By the second half of the twentieth century, vice presidents such as Richard M. Nixon, Hubert H. Humphrey, and Nelson A. Rockefeller, were such successful team players that they were no longer seen as

The vice president now has a working office in the White House, and a ceremonial office—Room 274 of the the Old Executive Office Building, pictured here.

officers of the Senate and came instead to be regarded as valued members of the executive branch. Symbolically, the office of the vice president was moved from the Senate to the Executive Office Building in the 1960s, and to the West Wing of the White House in the 1970s.

The development and growth of the vice presidency has been uneven because many nineteenth and early-twentieth-century vice presidents failed to develop satisfactory working relationships with their presidents or preferred to remain on the sidelines. A few, however, were willing to support their running mates, and they took the first steps toward enlarging the vice president's role in politics and government. For example, Democrat Martin Van Buren lived up to his nickname, the Little Magician, by working behind the scenes to engineer President Andrew Jackson's second-term victory as well as his own election as vice president. Van Buren, eager to launch his own presidential campaign in 1836, needed to stay in Jackson's good graces since the party would let the president choose his own successor. To this end, he publicly backed Jackson's stands on controversial issues such as nullification and abolition of the national bank, even though he privately disagreed with the president's positions. As presiding officer of the Senate, however, he could not defend the president's program since he was not permitted to participate in the proceedings. He recognized speakers and occasionally ruled on points of order during hot-tempered debates over Jackson's controversial programs; but during the most heated exchanges, he sat calmly reading a novel. Van Buren's fence-straddling strategy evidently worked; his election to the presidency was the last time the public so rewarded a vice president until the victory of George Bush in 1988.

Casting tiebreakers was one of the few traditional powers loyal nineteenth-century vice presidents could use to help presidents turn their programs into law. On one dramatic occasion, Vice President George M. Dallas put aside his personal preferences and broke a 27–27 tie to pass the controversial Walker Tariff of 1846, which President James K. Polk wanted. The tariff promoted free trade by reducing fees charged on foreign goods sold in the United States. It was unpopular in the North, particularly in Dallas's home state of Pennsylvania, where manufacturers wanted protection from overseas competition. Dallas justified his decision claiming that "the Vice President, now called upon to act, is a direct agent and representative of the whole people."[1] His deciding vote sparked such violent protests in Pennsylvania that he sent the Senate's sergeant-at-arms to Philadelphia to bring his wife and children to the capital for their safety.

The relationship between Democrats Polk and Dallas was so congenial that Dallas became the first

*L*incoln's first vice president, Hannibal Hamlin,
in a portrait by Matthew Brady, a photographer
who became famous for his pictures of the
Civil War and of President Lincoln

vice president after Van Buren to be kept up-to-date on
the president's policies and plans. Polk even asked for
Dallas's opinions on issues including the war with
Mexico and slavery. He also solicited the vice president's
comments on early drafts of his speeches. Neither president nor vice president chose to run for a second term.

Republican Hannibal Hamlin of Maine, Abraham
Lincoln's first vice president, was eager to serve his
president. Although the two men had never met,
Lincoln invited Hamlin to Chicago right after their election in 1860 and let him pick a member of the Cabinet.
He chose Gideon Welles for secretary of the navy.
Hamlin's handling of another prospective Cabinet
member, William H. Seward, cooled relations between
president and vice president for a time. Seward, Lincoln's

long-time political foe, had announced his retirement from the Senate, so the president made him an offer to become secretary of state as a gesture of party unity. Lincoln reluctantly sent Hamlin with a letter of appointment to see Seward, expecting the senator to turn it down. Much to Lincoln's dismay, Hamlin actually convinced Seward to accept the post. After bungling that delicate mission, Hamlin was to complain "I am not consulted at all, nor do I think there is much disposition . . . to regard any counsel I may give."[2] Yet, Lincoln took his vice president's advice on arming black troops to serve in the Union Army and even read him a draft of the Emancipation Proclamation in the fall of 1862. In 1864, Hamlin, a dedicated abolitionist, spent the summer as a private in the Maine Coast Guard, the only vice president to serve while holding office. Because Lincoln wanted to attract southern and border votes, Hamlin was not nominated for a second term.

Garret A. Hobart anticipated twentieth-century vice presidents by serving as a very effective congressional liaison for Republican President William McKinley. A self-made man of enormous wealth, Hobart took up residence in the Tayloe Mansion, within walking distance of the White House. There he proceeded to give "smokers," inviting members of Congress for drinks and card games. McKinley was a frequent visitor, and both he and his vice president used these informal occasions to sway votes in favor of the president's policies. Despite his skill in influencing politicians, Hobart still had to cast a crucial tiebreaker in the Senate. President McKinley decided that the United States should annex the Philippine Islands, a former Spanish possession that was turned over to the United States in the aftermath of the Spanish-American War of 1898. The nation's leading politicians and intellectuals were bitterly divided over the wisdom of the annexation, but Hobart went ahead and voted against a resolution to grant the Philippines freedom, postponing their independence for another fifty years.

McKinley was one of the few presidents to publicly acknowledge his vice president's contributions to his administration. At the president's first state dinner, he treated the vice president as his guest of honor, not the British ambassador, as was expected. Hobart was so helpful to McKinley that he was often referred to as the "Assistant President."[3] During the Spanish-American War, McKinley had even invited him to sit in on Cabinet meetings, a practice that had long fallen into disuse and would be sporadically revived and abandoned over the next three decades. Hobart's heavy schedule of entertaining and work may have been a factor leading to his death from a heart attack before he completed his term.

The election of Democrat Franklin D. Roosevelt in 1932 permanently altered the vice presidency. During his unprecedented four terms as president, Roosevelt faced two major challenges: directing the recovery of the economy from the Great Depression, and then supervising the American war effort during World War II. To meet these challenges, the president and Congress expanded the scope and functions of the national government, including the duties assigned to the vice president. As a result, presiding over the Senate and casting tiebreakers became minor aspects of the vice presidential job description.

During his first term as vice president, before disagreements marred his relationship with the president (see Chapter 5), John Nance Garner was an active member of the Roosevelt team and was given more responsibility than any previous vice president. As a former Speaker of the House, Garner was well suited to serve as the president's liaison to Congress. He wandered around the Senate floor during debate, seeking out undecided lawmakers and getting them to vote as the president wished. He kept a private, liquor-stocked office, called the Board of Education, where he entertained senators in an effort to persuade them to cooperate with the administration, much as Hobart had. At his suggestion, Roosevelt instituted weekly meetings with congressional leaders to discuss his policies, a practice continued by later presidents. Even though Garner did not always approve of the legislation Roosevelt sponsored, he was consulted as it was formulated, and if he could not get it modified, he loyally supported it.

Although Adams, Hobart, Marshall, and Coolidge had sporadically attended Cabinet meetings in the past, Garner was the first vice president to become a regular member of the presidential advisory group, a practice continued by all of his successors. He never hesitated to state his opinions even when these were not popular. Garner was also the first vice president to travel outside the United States in an official capacity. In Japan he was received by Emperor Hirohito. He visited the Philippines in his capacity as president of the Senate and attended the opening of the Inter-American highway in Mexico as a goodwill ambassador. Despite his achievements in office, Garner complained that the vice presidency was "not worth a bucket of warm spit."[4]

Roosevelt's second vice president, the liberal Henry A. Wallace, was also sent on trips abroad—even before he was sworn in. The Spanish-speaking vice president-elect attended the inauguration of Mexican president Avila Camacho in December 1940. He went on a goodwill tour of Latin American countries as the president's representative in March 1943. Finally, in 1944 he traveled to the Far East for two months, carrying messages to Chinese leader Chiang Kai-shek, and reporting back to the president on the conditions he found. Wallace's foreign-policy pronouncements did not endear him to Congress because he was considered pro-Soviet and

*Vice President Henry Wallace (left) and Madame
and Marshal Chiang Kai-shek drink a toast to the
success of the United Nations during Wallace's
visit to the Chinese leader in 1944.*

he underestimated the Soviet Union's tyranny over its
citizens. Further, he was an internationalist long before
most Americans realized that the United States would
have to become more involved in world affairs. His concern for workers' living standards and conditions of
employment in other countries was not shared by
Congress, either.

It was not, however, as a roving ambassador, but
as an administrator that Wallace made his mark on the
vice presidency. Wallace was in a unique position to
help the president because he had served as secretary
of agriculture and knew how Cabinet departments were
run. During the summer of 1941, Roosevelt chose
Wallace to become the chairman of the newly formed
Economic Defense Board, assigned to stockpile stra-
tegic supplies the nation might need if it entered World
War II. Wallace was in charge of eight heads of govern-

ment departments and a staff of about three thousand. In December 1941, when the United States was drawn into the conflict, the organization was renamed the Board of Economic Warfare (BEW) and was also given responsibility for postwar economic planning.

When he set up government agencies and coordinating groups, Roosevelt rarely drew clear lines of authority. This is why Wallace inevitably came into conflict with Jesse Jones, administrator of the Reconstruction Finance Corporation, and Cordell Hull, the secretary of state, over their respective jurisdictions as well as over matters of policy. Their disputes created more problems for Roosevelt to solve. Finally, in July 1943, the president set up a new organization to replace the BEW and relieved Jones and Wallace of responsibility for international economic procurement. Despite setbacks, Wallace's eighteen months as a vice presidential administrator set a precedent for his successors. For political reasons, he was dropped from the ticket when Roosevelt ran for a fourth term (see Chapter 6).

During the Cold War era, a time of tense relations with the Soviet Union accompanied by the fear of nuclear war, vice presidents were expected to help evaluate and guard the nation's security, to be constantly informed about world events, and to be prepared to assume the presidency if needed. This is why President Harry S. Truman, who was singularly unprepared to take over the presidency in 1945, asked Congress to make the vice president a statutory member of the National Security Council (NSC). It was created in 1947 to monitor possible threats to the United States from abroad. Seventy-one-year-old Vice President Alben W. Barkley, a fellow Democrat and pal from Truman's Senate days, duly attended meetings of the NSC, but seemed indifferent to the assignment. Since he had no desire to make policy or advise the president, his presence at NSC and Cabinet meetings contributed little of substance.

Barkley was happiest in his ceremonial role as the president's representative, and his appearances around the nation endeared him to the public.

> *I suppose I traveled, mostly by air, more than any Vice President had up to that time, making speeches in all parts of the country. Many of these speeches were semi-official in nature, for I often represented the President, who, naturally, was limited in his ability to accept engagements. . . .*
>
> *Of course, for a certain period, I seemed to be much in demand as a crowner of "queens" at various celebrations—Apple Blossom festivals, Cherry Blossom festivals and just about every sort of festival that one can think of. It seemed an inevitable— and not entirely unwelcome—part of the ritual that the visiting Vice President should kiss the queen after crowning her.[5]*

Barkley's ten years as Senate majority leader made him an effective spokesman for Truman's policies in Congress, and he was often able to serve as a link between the Capitol and the White House. Nevertheless, he realized that a vice president had to respect the senate's independence and its resentment of executive interference. "Undoubtedly, a Vice-President who is well liked by members of the Senate . . . can exercise considerable power in the shaping of the program of legislation which every administration seeks to enact."[6] While presiding over the Senate, Barkley, a widower, often dashed off letters to Jane Hadley, whom he married in 1949. He commented, "I would have done anything, even the most outrageous sort of filibuster, to keep the senators talking so I could get my love letters written."[7] In 1952, he was considered too old to run for the presidency, although that had long been his dream, and he retired from politics.

Republican President Dwight D. Eisenhower's running mate, Richard M. Nixon, was an example of a vice president who played an effective political role as an aggressive campaigner. Repeating his 1952 performance (see Chapter 4), he became Eisenhower's "hit man" during the midterm elections of 1954, preserving the president's image as an affable leader of all the people. Nixon blasted the opposition, accusing the Democratic party of corruption in government and labeling its candidates as soft on communism. He traveled over 26,000 miles, visiting 95 cities in 31 states, giving 204 speeches and more than 100 press conferences.[8] Although the Republicans lost their majorities in Congress, Nixon's performance showed how successful vice presidents could be in building party unity, raising campaign funds, and creating political IOUs for their own future campaigns.

Nixon also proved how useful a vice president could be when a president was disabled (see Chapter 7), and he brought further recognition to his office when he visited foreign nations on behalf of the president as Garner and Wallace had before him. The vice president made seven trips outside the United States, the most dramatic in 1958 when hostile mobs in Lima, Peru, and Caracas, Venezuela, booed his speeches, surrounded his car, and threw rocks at him. The confrontations received worldwide coverage and gave him a reputation for courage under fire as well as the highest public-approval ratings of his career.[9] In 1959, his image as an anticommunist foreign-policy spokesperson was given a tremendous boost when he met Soviet leader Nikita S. Khrushchev at the opening of the first American exhibition in Moscow. While the two men toured an American model home, they stopped in the kitchen and engaged in a heated discussion of the advantages

149

of their systems of government. "Isn't it better to be talking about the relative merits of our washing machines than the relative strength of our rockets?"[10] Nixon insisted. The "kitchen debate" did not resolve any of the important issues dividing the United States and the Soviet Union, but it did focus attention on the vice president and bring him more respect. Nevertheless, he was defeated in the 1960 election and did not become president until 1969.

As Lyndon B. Johnson's vice president, Hubert H. Humphrey was a model of loyalty and discretion, but, like Vice President Dallas, he paid a high price for being such a dedicated team player. His close friendship with Johnson began when the two Democrats entered the Senate in 1948, but was sorely tested by Johnson's unexpected insensitivity when president. For example, in front of reporters at Johnson's Texas ranch, the president had Humphrey don an outsized Western outfit and mount a spirited horse which he could hardly ride. Humphrey liked to talk—about everything, all the time. "I do—I like every subject. I can't help it," he explained; but his constant enthusiasm and incessant chatter got on Johnson's nerves to such a point that the president commented, "If I could just breed him to Calvin Coolidge. . . ."[11]

Humphrey chaired more councils and commissions than any other vice president, but these produced studies, not actions, and were just make-work projects to keep him occupied. The vice president headed the Aeronautics and Space Council, the Councils on Economic Opportunity, Equal Opportunity, Marine Sciences, Recreation and Natural Beauty, Youth Opportunity, and Indian Opportunity, among others. It was as the president's liaison to Congress that Humphrey scored his greatest success. As a former senator, Humphrey respected Senate customs and knew his place. As he explained, "The Vice Presidency can work to strain the

Vice President Hubert Humphrey meets with President Johnson in the White House.

relationship between old friends in the Congress because you're no longer a member of the Club, and you're not quite out."[12] Such sensitivity helped him convince the lawmakers to pass the administration's Great Society legislation, including the president's Model Cities Program, Medicare, his Youth Opportunities Program, the creation of the Department of Housing and Urban Development, and the 1965 Voting Rights Act.

In 1965, Humphrey objected to Johnson's policy of increasing American involvement in the Vietnam War to help the South Vietnam government repel communist incursions from North Vietnam. Knowing that the president did not want him to express his opposition in public, the loyal vice president wrote a lengthy memo stating his position. Johnson was unhappy that Humphrey had put his concerns in writing rather than discussing them with him in person. As a result of his stand on Vietnam, Humphrey was excluded for a year from weekly lunches at the White House to discuss war policy. By 1966, he was reinstated at the lunches after he successfully completed a mission to convince Asian nations to accept the president's Vietnam policy. Humphrey paid a high price at the polls for his loyalty to Johnson when he ran for president in 1968. People had forgotten that he was the spokesman for the administration's popular domestic programs and condemned him for his failure to speak out in public against the controversial war in Vietnam. He began to call for a halt to the bombing of Communist-controlled North Vietnam in the last months of his campaign, but it was too little, too late, and the voters rejected him.

Republican Vice President Spiro T. Agnew was most effective as a political spokesperson for President Nixon's administration. He was often called "Nixon's Nixon"[13] for his hard-hitting rhetoric. He lashed out at students protesting the Vietnam War and accused them of being "spoiled brats who never had a good spanking."[14] Agnew vehemently criticized permissiveness in American society and argued for a restoration of law and order. He also took on the media as a "gaggle of commentators" who "bask in their own provincialism, their own parochialism."[15] His speeches appealed to Americans who opposed civil rights, feared student unrest, and were suspicious of the nation's intellectuals. He used colorful (and offensive) phrases like "effete corps of impudent snobs,"[16] and racial and ethnic slurs, referring to a "Polack," and a "fat Jap."[17] During the midterm elections of 1970, he embarked on an ideological campaign to drive liberals from government. One of the victims of his invective was Senator Charles Goodall of New York, a Republican, who was defeated for reelection. Nixon could have denied that Agnew's remarks represented his views, but he never did.

The vice president was singularly ineffective as presiding officer of the Senate, for, like Henry Wallace, he had never served in that legislative body. As the former governor of Maryland, he knew little about Senate customs and procedures. While he sought the senators' goodwill by lunching and talking with them, his efforts to get them to change their votes in favor of administration policies proved disastrous. In 1969, he buttonholed Senator Len Jordan of Idaho to get him to support an administration tax proposal. However, the vice president had violated Senate custom, which discouraged such lobbying tactics in the Senate chamber just before a roll-call vote. Agnew was told that although the senator had planned to support the president, he would no longer do so because Agnew had violated Senate traditions. At the next meeting of Republican senators, the senator presented "Jordan's rule" to his colleagues: to vote the other way if the vice president tried to lobby a senator on the floor of the Senate.[18] From then on, Agnew's influence on Capitol Hill waned (see Chapter 4).

To get Nelson Rockefeller to agree to become an appointive vice president in 1974, Republican President Gerald Ford had to make a number of important concessions to him. Rockefeller wanted to be Ford's domestic advisor, so he was made vice chairman of the Domestic Council. In that post, the vice president expected to oversee White House staffers and department heads, determine which problems would receive the president's attention, and formulate solutions to them. His staff was increased from seventy to eighty-four so that he would have people available to do research on the projects and programs that he wanted to present to the president. To his disappointment, the vice president soon discovered that the Domestic Council was designed to coordinate policy within the executive branch, not to make it.

Not since Henry Wallace had a vice president been given such an important policy position, and, like Wallace, Rockefeller ran into difficulties arising from executive-branch rivalries and from the perception that he was too liberal. White House chief of staff Donald Rumsfeld, protective of his own influence with the president, and conservative members of the White House staff who objected to the vice president's spending programs, undermined Rockefeller's authority on the council. For example, they cut him off from the flow of information circulating within the White House. Rockefeller grew frustrated and left the council at the end of 1975.

Rockefeller had also been asked to chair a commission to investigate the activities of the Central Intelligence Agency (CIA), which had been compromised during the Watergate scandal. The CIA investigation proved to be a ticklish assignment. If Rockefeller failed to find fault with the spy organization, liberals in Congress would accuse him of whitewashing the CIA, but if he condemned it too severely, conservatives would object. In the end, his report antagonized both groups.

Vice President Nelson Rockefeller sits at his office desk in the Capitol for the first time in December 1974.

Like Wallace and Agnew, Rockefeller, the former governor of New York, had never been a United States Senator. His lack of familiarity with Senate traditions and his commitment to liberalism made him a controversial presiding officer. Early on, he was asked for a procedural ruling on cloture, the vote taken to end lengthy filibusters, a cause dear to Senate liberals. He offended conservatives by deciding that a motion to take up changes in a rule, such as the existing cloture rule, could be made by a simple majority vote, not a two-thirds vote. This made it easier for Senate liberals to alter the cloture rule, reducing the number of votes required to invoke it from two-thirds to three-fifths of the senators. Rockefeller further antagonized the Senate during debates when he failed to recognize important conservatives who wished to speak, such as James B. Allen of Alabama, to whom he later apologized.[19]

Unlike his predecessors, the vice president had demanded and been given the right to meet privately

155

with the president once a week. Rockefeller used these sessions to interest Ford in his pet projects, including the Energy Independent Authority, a research and development program to make the United States independent of foreign sources of energy. At this time, a number of oil-producing nations were refusing to sell petroleum to the United States, causing an energy crisis. Rockefeller's influence with the president waned, however, as Ford returned to his more conservative roots. Because of the vice president's demonstrated liberalism, he was dropped from the ticket when Ford decided to run for president in 1976. In summing up his experience, Rockefeller said, "For me, these past two years, in all candor, cannot be said to have sorely tried either my talents or my stamina."[20]

"Outsider" President Jimmy Carter, formerly a Georgia governor, put former Minnesota senator Walter F. Mondale's knowledge of Washington, D.C., to good use, and made him one of the most influential vice presidents in modern history. Carter praised him, stating, "There is not a single aspect of my own responsibilities in which Fritz [Mondale] is not intimately associated. He is the only person that I have, with both the substantive knowledge and political stature to whom I can turn over a major assignment."[21] As early as the election campaign, Democrat Mondale began setting precedents. He was the first vice president to participate in a televised debate with his opponent, Republican Senator Bob Dole. After Mondale was sworn in, he was given an office in the West Wing of the White House, near the president's Oval Office, and held weekly private meetings with Carter. In addition, he was invited to sit in on any White House meetings he chose to attend and had access to the same information the president received, including national-security briefings.

Mondale asked the president to relieve him from serving as a liaison with Congress to avoid possible conflicts with the White House staff member Frank Moore, whose duty that was. The vice president's staff was integrated with the White House staff to encourage cooperation between them. Unlike Humphrey and Rockefeller, Mondale avoided assignments to head commissions because they diverted his staff from policy research and encouraged jealousies and competition within the executive branch. Also, as he explained, "I think, in the past, Vice Presidents have often taken on minor functions in order to make it appear that their role was significant. . . . "[22]

Mondale concentrated instead on advising the president and helping him plan his long-range agenda. Like Vice President Hamlin, he was consulted on Cabinet appointments, and he was instrumental in getting Joseph Califano named secretary of the Department of Health, Education, and Welfare. While he rarely advocated specific policies, he was involved in decisions to reorganize the intelligence agencies, establish a separate Department of Education, return the Panama Canal to Panama, and expand child-welfare programs, among others. Instead of presenting proposals at meetings, he listened to what others had to say and then approached Carter privately to express his views. Because he stayed in the background and quietly advised the president, Mondale's disagreements with Carter were not made public. In 1984, he admitted that he had objected to a number of the president's actions, including the selling of F-15 fighter jets to Saudi Arabia, his seclusion during the Iranian hostage crisis in 1980, and the imposition of a grain embargo on the Soviet Union after its invasion of Afghanistan.[23] Mondale had even defended the administration's controversial grain embargo during the 1980 presidential campaign.

Like his predecessors, the vice president traveled extensively on the president's behalf. He made fourteen overseas trips in all, compared with six for Rockefeller, one for Ford, seven for Agnew, twelve for Humphrey, and ten for Johnson.[24] In addition to state funerals and goodwill tours, Mondale performed substantive diplomatic duties for the president. During a 1977 visit to the Middle East, he worked on the Egyptian-Israeli peace plan that led to the Camp David Accords in 1978 and an eventual peace treaty. He also took to the road during midterm elections in 1978 and made a hundred speeches in twenty states,[25] but failed to stem the tide of voter dissatisfaction with the Carter administration. In the election of 1980, the Carter-Mondale team was soundly defeated by popular Republicans Ronald Reagan and George Bush. Mondale's own bid for the presidency in 1984 met a similar fate.

As Ronald Reagan's vice president, George Bush followed the path Walter Mondale had charted, advising the president privately while supporting and defending him publicly. He met with the president for weekly lunches, received daily national security briefings, and even occupied the office Mondale had used. He led task forces investigating the serial murders of children in Atlanta, and seeking ways to eliminate excessive government regulations, a project dear to Reagan Republicans, and he was named head of the president's crisis-management team (later called the Special Situations Group), to coordinate government responses to foreign and domestic emergencies such as terrorist attacks. In view of Bush's background as director of the CIA, UN representative, and chief of the U.S. Liaison Office in China, he was effective as a presidential emissary to other nations. He also traveled around the United States during midterm elections, supporting his party's candidates and raising money for them.

Because of his unquestioning public acceptance of President Reagan's policies, Vice President Bush was haunted by the "wimp factor," as a vice president who would do anything to please his boss. He defended Reagan's economic program, which he had scorned when opposing Reagan in the presidential primaries (see Chapter 3). He tried to stay out of the headlines and serve as a self-effacing team player. As he explained, "If I'm out there with a high profile, holding press conferences, putting my spin on whatever it is, I won't have a [good] relationship with the President."[26] He kept such a low profile that no one could pin any blame on him when the Iran-Contra scandal broke, exposing NSC members who sold arms to Iran and used the proceeds to fund insurgents trying to topple the left-wing government in Nicaragua. To this day, it is uncertain how much he knew about what was going on and when he knew it. By closely associating himself with the popular president, in 1988 Bush became the first vice president since Van Buren to win election as president.

At age forty-two, youthful Dan Quayle was supposed to follow the pattern set by the older George Bush as vice president, but he chose to become more visible than his predecessor. Unlike Bush, he spoke up at Cabinet meetings and often took issue with experienced department heads. He urged the president to go public with his foreign-policy actions to build support for them. However, his own public misstatements and gaffes embarrassed the administration both at home and abroad (see Chapter 3). Many people were disturbed at the prospect of Quayle's becoming president when Bush was briefly hospitalized for a heart irregularity in May 1991. A *New York Times*–CBS News poll found that only 19 percent of those polled had a favorable opinion of the vice president and 62 percent worried about his serving as president.[27] Quayle confessed that "the job of the Vice President is an awkward one. There is no doubt about it that there is some frustration, but having said that, I love this job and I love working for this President."[28]

Behind the scenes, Quayle, a former senator from Indiana, was a successful congressional liaison and even managed to get the lawmakers to approve a redesigned space station, despite objections from the National Academy of Sciences. In the midterm elections, he launched a bitterly partisan campaign, reminiscent of Nixon and Agnew, and visited fifty states, raising more than fifteen million dollars.[29] He performed well, even though the Republicans lost seats in Congress. In the 1992 presidential race, President Bush stood by Quayle despite pressure to remove him from the ticket. Quayle's most memorable contribution to the Bush campaign was his introduction of a "family values" issue, but he was ridiculed because he attacked a television character, Murphy Brown, for glamorizing single parenthood instead of addressing the problems of actual people. The Bush-Quayle team lost the election of 1992, and Quayle's hopes of running for president himself in the 1996 race faded as a result of health and fund-raising problems.

Like Democrats Mondale and Carter, "insider" Vice President Al Gore, a former senator from Tennessee, and "outsider" President Bill Clinton, the recent governor of Arkansas, developed a close working relationship based on mutual respect. Both men were of the baby-boomer generation and southerners, which also helped them to get along. To ensure that the presidential and vice presidential staffs would function well together, Gore's chief of staff also served as an assistant to the president. Gore provided the key to his and Clinton's success as a team with the statement: "My principal goal is to help the President do the best he possibly can, and so my own record as Vice-President is necessarily obscured, in significant measure because so much of my energy goes into trying to help him."[30] The vice president proved very helpful indeed. Not only did

The prospect of an unprepared, or inadequate, vice president having to step up to the presidency has been the subject of much rueful humor.

he have knowledge of Washington politics that the president lacked, he also had a complementary approach to government problems. While Clinton tended to debate all aspects of an issue without coming to a conclusion, Gore was focused, and encouraged his chief to make a decision and take action. The two men did not always agree; for example, Gore favored the use of punitive air strikes against the warring Serbs in Bosnia to bring them to the peace table, a course which the president found unacceptable. Nevertheless, Gore earned Clinton's respect because he voiced his criticisms of the president's policies in private.

Gore worked quietly behind the scenes in foreign policy. His numerous trips abroad were not just ceremonial in nature, for he managed to develop an infor-

*Vice presidential candidate Al Gore, with
Bill Clinton behind him, speaks to a crowd at a
campaign stop in the 1992 election.*

mal channel with Russian leaders outside of diplomatic circles to make the Russian government more
aware of the administration's views. Gore was thereby
able to negotiate a top-secret deal with Russia and
Kazakhstan to bring bomb-grade uranium to the United States. He also developed channels to the South
African and Egyptian governments with the blessing
of the president and Secretary of State Warren
Christopher.

During his first two years in office, Gore was also
involved in domestic politics. Like Vice President
Hamlin, Gore was consulted on Cabinet appointments.
Although he had his share of defeats in Congress as
the president's liaison, he managed to push through
the North American Free Trade Agreement after debating one of its more vocal opponents, H. Ross Perot, on

"The Larry King Show." Appearances with Larry King and on "The Late Show with David Letterman" helped the vice president overcome his somewhat colorless, wooden manner before the public.

During Gore's first two years in office, his domestic policy assignments included development of the information superhighway, to increase access to the flow of communication; empowerment zones to help disadvantaged city neighborhoods; and environmental controls to reduce pollution, a longstanding interest of Gore's. The vice president also recommended measures to reinvent the government, decentralizing and streamlining government agencies. As a loyal vice president, he took the assignments he was given and managed them with enthusiasm, even though they were often overshadowed by more controversial programs such as the Clinton administration's ill-fated health-care reforms. Gore had wanted to work on this problem, but it was given to the president's wife, Hillary. After the Republican midterm election victory, the administration, eager to pare down government expenses, began to reconsider Gore's decentralization plan.

As loyal team players, vice presidents have taken on a variety of assignments and became established members of the executive branch. They have welcomed additional responsibilities only to have their recommendations ignored, to compete with rivals within the White House for access to the president, to risk having presidents disavow their statements, and occasionally to have presidents take away their hard-won assignments. Too infrequently have they been praised for their achievements, but then, vice presidents have been expected to keep out of the spotlight, leaving the public and even party leaders unaware of their many accomplishments. Perhaps, the time has come to rethink the role of the vice president and reinvent its purpose within the executive branch of the government.

Reinventing the Government: Proposals to Reform the Vice Presidency

There should be no legislation nor any constitutional amendment giving the office of the Vice President more power. . . . So far as the law is concerned, one man should run the executive branch of the Government, not two.

Henry Wallace

OVER THE YEARS, THE VICE PRESIDENCY HAS BEEN CRITICIZED as an afterthought, a convenient solution to an electoral problem that no longer exists, and as an appendage to government, lacking meaningful constitutional functions. Solutions to these flaws have divided reformers into two camps. Some would simply abolish the vice presidency. They remember that the office of vice president has been vacant during eighteen administrations due to the deaths of seven occupants, the elevation to the presidency of nine others, and the resignation of two more. Other reformers urge that the vice president's legal and constitutional tasks be increased. They recall that a number of modern vice presidents, including John N. Garner, Henry A. Wallace, Hubert H. Humphrey, Walter F. Mondale, and Albert Gore, took on additional duties with some success.

164

The selection process, too, has been a separate target of criticism. The Twelfth Amendment reduced the likelihood that the nation would be governed by presidents and vice presidents from two different parties. Nevertheless, the process has not prevented the election of officials representing opposing wings of a party, like James A. Garfield and Chester A. Arthur, nor has it kept temperamentally incompatible pairs, like Calvin Coolidge and Charles G. Dawes, from office. Also, it has failed to screen candidates for private problems, or for financial misconduct. While the Twenty-fifth Amendment may have corrected the problems of presidential disabilities and vice presidential vacancies, it, too, produced an unexpected and unsatisfactory result, the nation's only unelected president and vice president, Gerald R. Ford and Nelson A. Rockefeller. These flaws triggered demands for further reforms.

Some members of Congress first proposed abolishing the office of vice president in 1803, during debates on the Twelfth Amendment. From their point of view, the vice presidency had been created simply to make the electoral system work by increasing the pool of qualified candidates. Under the proposed Twelfth Amendment, vice presidents would no longer serve this purpose. In addition, separate balloting for president and vice president would rule out the hope of first-runner-up-status in presidential elections and thus fewer outstanding candidates would be attracted to the race. Senator Jonathan Dayton of New Jersey summarized his objections to continuing the vice presidency stating, "The reasons for erecting the office are frustrated by the amendment. . . . It will be preferable, therefore, to abolish the office."[1] The Senate voted down his proposal 19–12. In the House, Representative Samuel W. Dana of Connecticut adopted a similar line of argument, and the House rejected his motion by a vote of 85–27.

In the mid-1980s, historian Arthur Schlesinger, Jr., echoed Dayton's and Dana's sentiments when he pronounced the office superfluous,[2] a view supported by a survey of the vice president's constitutional duties. One of those duties is to preside over the Senate. As early as 1803, Representative Roger Griswold of Connecticut had noticed that the Senate "sit half their time without the Vice President, and I have not understood that the business is not as well done without him as with him."[3] The situation has not changed very much in modern times; for example, Vice President Mondale spent only nineteen days of his first year in office presiding over the Senate, for a total of eighteen hours.[4] In fact, the task is so undemanding that when the vice president is absent, the president pro tempore, usually a senior senator from the majority party with important committee assignments to fulfill, often delegates this responsibility to a junior senator.

While the presiding officer is called upon to give rulings on Senate procedures, the parliamentarian usually provides guidance; and no matter what a vice president decides, the Senate may overrule the decision. As Vice President Calvin Coolidge put it, "At first I intended to become a student of the Senate rules and I did learn much about them, but I soon found that the Senate had but one fixed rule, subject to exceptions, of course, which was to the effect that the Senate would do anything it wanted to do whenever it wanted to do it."[5] The vice president's responsibility for casting a tie-breaking vote has also fallen into disuse. For example, even with a Senate almost equally divided between the two parties during the first six years of his vice presidency, Richard M. Nixon had to break only eight ties in eight years.[6] Since Senate voting is scheduled in advance and party leaders keep count of the votes they can muster, vice presidents can always be notified of a possible tie vote and come to the Senate when needed—

unless, like Vice President Charles G. Dawes, they go off for a long nap and take too long to return.

The vice president's most important constitutional responsibility is to serve as a potential presidential successor; but the framers of the Constitution had intended the vice president to serve only as acting president until the following November, when another, special presidential election could be arranged. This is why Schlesinger does not feel that the succession problem should stand in the way of eliminating the vice presidency. He argues that if there were no longer a vice presidency, the secretary of state could be empowered to serve as acting president for ninety days until a special election were held to choose a new president.[7] A Cabinet official, as interim president, could avoid problems of partisanship that would inevitably occur if the presidency were in the hands of one party and Congress in the hands of the other.

Among the possible objections to this scheme that Schlesinger attempts to dispel is the idea that the vice president is the only other government official elected by the whole nation and should therefore remain the president's designated successor. He argues, "No one votes for a Vice President. He is part of a package deal."[8] During campaigns, attention is directed toward presidential nominees, not their running mates, and vice presidents seem to have had minimal impact on election returns even in their home states. Nor should the vice presidency be seen as a training ground for the presidency, making these officeholders seem better qualified than other possible successors. John Tyler, Andrew Johnson, and Harry Truman had very little on-the-job training before they were called upon to lead the nation. Furthermore, vice presidents may privately disagree with their predecessors' policies and not wish to be bound by them as president. As Vice President Thomas Marshall pointed out, "A Vice-President might make a poor President, but he would make a much poorer one if he attempted to subordinate his own mind and views to carry out the ideas of a dead man."[9] In sum, the vice president may have no special qualifications or claim to fill a presidential vacancy other than a constitutional requirement, and an amendment could take care of that.

As attractive as the idea may seem to some people, it is unlikely that the vice presidency will be abolished. For better or worse, the office has been part of the national heritage for over two hundred years, and there are no compelling reasons to eliminate it now, especially since its recent occupants have become increasingly visible to the public, have taken on more responsibilities, and have become a popular source of presidential candidates. The vice president has played an increasingly important role in providing stability and continuity during national traumas, as evidenced by the smooth transition that followed the assassination of President Kennedy and the uninterrupted functioning of government during the illnesses of Presidents Eisenhower and Reagan. Modern vice presidents are in a unique position to take over when called upon since they have access to most, if not all, of the information that reaches the president's desk and sit-in on briefings and policy-making meetings. If the vice presidency were as insignificant as some critics claim, Congress would not have chosen to pass the Twenty-fifth Amendment to fill vice presidential vacancies nor have given the vice president an important role during presidential disabilities.

Those who value the office would give its occupants an even more substantial role in government, but defining that role presents problems. By law, modern vice presidents are members of the National Security Council, the Smithsonian Board of Regents, and the National Aeronautics and Space Council. Presidents have assigned them other duties as heads of commissions, overseas emissaries, and policy advisors. To carry out these tasks, vice presidents have been given their own staffs and budgets, offices in the White House, and easy access to presidents and to the information they receive (see Chapter 8). This may serve to give vice presidents more public recognition and personal comfort, but not necessarily more power.

It has been argued that the additional assignments are only make-work projects to keep vice presidents busy[10] and may be handed out or taken back as the president sees fit. Nevertheless, two former presidents, Herbert Hoover and Gerald Ford, have recommended that the vice president become more helpful to the overburdened modern president. With the decline of political parties, a longer campaign season, frequent stalemates in Congress, and the demands of world leadership, the president's job has become even more exhausting and complicated. Herbert Hoover proposed the creation of a second, administrative, vice president, appointed by the president and approved by the Senate, to oversee the president's staff.[11] Gerald Ford suggested that the vice president become a chief of staff to control the administration bureaucracy and improve relations with Congress.[12] Hoover's idea was rejected because it would leave the constitutional vice president with even less to do. Since other officials, such as the White House chief of staff, were already performing the functions Mr. Hoover and Mr. Ford had in mind, no formal action has been taken on their recommendations.

Other proposals to give the incumbent vice president more formal duties, such as supervision of a Cabinet department, are also problematic since vice presidents might have to defend their turf and disagree with the president in public. Unlike other Cabinet officers, presidents could not fire them for insubordination or incompetence. Also, handling a Cabinet post would absorb vice presidential energies and leave little time for other duties. As Vice President Dan Quayle put it, "A vice president is a vice president. . . . He's got to know everything that's going on, not just one special area."[13] More importantly, such schemes would probably run counter to Article II of the Constitution, which prevents the delegation of executive power to any other independent government official. Vice President Henry Wallace explained the situation in practical terms, "There should be no legislation nor any constitutional amendment giving the office of the Vice President more power. . . . So far as the law is concerned, one man should run the executive branch of the Government, not two."[14]

With these considerations in mind, the Twentieth Century Fund Task Force on the Vice Presidency has proposed that vice presidents continue to receive unlimited access to information as well as the resources necessary to prepare them for the presidency and go on serving primarily as presidential advisors. In the opinion of the task force, whatever additional duties presidents choose to assign, such as acting as administration spokesperson or diplomatic envoy, should not conflict with this, the vice president's most important role. Members of the task force concluded that no rigid rules should govern the duties the president assigns the vice president because their working relationship will depend on "their temperaments, experiences, and strengths as well as their views of executive leadership."[15] How successful their working relationship becomes will, to a large extent, depend on the kind of person chosen to serve as vice president.

Each of the numerous suggestions for improving the vice presidential selection process has different strengths and weaknesses because the reforms must address a series of overlapping and sometimes conflicting problems. These include (1) finding sufficient time to investigate prospective nominees' backgrounds and choosing a qualified candidate; (2) making a choice that will increase party unity and party democracy, giving ordinary delegates or even voters a voice in the nomination process; (3) selecting a nominee who will balance the ticket and widen the party's appeal to voters; (4) assuring some measure of personal compatibility with the presidential candidate. Unfortunately, no one reform can treat all these concerns.

To allow time for thorough background checks and to find a compatible partner for the president, the party convention schedule could be changed to encourage the screening of prospective vice presidents; however, a few days might not be sufficient, and a prolonged convention schedule might cause delegates to lose interest, enthusiasm, and momentum. The president could also select a vice president after the election, and submit the name to Congress for approval; but party unity, ticket balancing, and party democracy would be sacrificed and, more importantly, the constitutional provisions for a popularly elected vice president would be violated. Alternatively, the president could select a running mate before the election for approval by party officials of the national committee, the party's executive body; but this, too, might weaken party unity and party democracy. The presidential candidate could also preselect a vice presidential nominee so that the two could run as a team in primaries. This approach would further strengthen party democracy by letting ordinary party members, not just delegates, participate in the selection process, but it could jeopardize party unity if primaries revealed splits within the party. Also, contenders for the presidential nomination might not wish to settle for the vice presidency prematurely, which would make it difficult to recruit top candidates for the post.

Other proposals have different drawbacks. To increase party unity and balance the ticket, the vice presidential nominee might be chosen in an open contest

171

during the convention, but it would be difficult to allow for careful background checks and consideration of ticket compatibility. To get qualified candidates, a vice presidential candidate might be selected from the party's top three presidential competitors after the presidential nomination was completed, although the running mates might not get along. To widen the party's appeal to voters, the whole ticket could be chosen on a national primary day, but this alternative would probably decrease chances for party unity, and could produce an unbalanced ticket or one of incompatible candidates. Breaking up the traditional tickets on the ballot to have separate national elections for the president and vice president would have similar drawbacks and the added complication that the victors might come from two different parties.

Perhaps the best solution to selection problems is the one that is gradually evolving. As primaries increasingly determine the choice of presidential candidates far in advance of party conventions, the nominees-to-be could use their time, as Jimmy Carter did, to interview and screen potential running mates. Even during the primary campaigns, reporters could persistently question presidential hopefuls about their prospective choices for vice president to keep the issue before them and before the public.[16] Although questions of party unity and ticket balancing would remain, they could be factored into the presidential candidates' decision since they might solicit party leaders' advice in recruiting and evaluating possible running mates.

The Twenty-fifth Amendment was designed to solve the problems of vice presidential vacancies and presidential disabilities, but the reforms it put in place have been criticized. As an unanticipated result of the amendment, the United States was governed by an unelected president and an unelected vice president from 1974 to 1976. This violated a basic tenet of American democracy by depriving voters of the right to choose their leaders. Perhaps the amendment should be changed to require a special national election to choose a president if a term of more than two years remained to be completed.[17] Another problem surfaced when Congress confirmed Ford as vice president in less than two months but took twice as long to approve Rockefeller's appointment. The delay allowed for Vice President Rockefeller's opponents on the president's staff to undermine him before he could even get down to work. If the two houses of Congress held a single joint hearing on the credentials of the vice presidential nominee, the confirmation process could be speeded up.[18]

The disability provisions of the amendment have created new concerns. Representative Henry B. Gonzalez of Texas warned about "the almost unchecked ease with which the President can be removed by either an unscrupulous or mistaken subordinate."[19] With a little imagination, it is possible to weave all manner of conspiracies involving a cast of characters from presidents' spouses and physicians to members of the White House staff; but only vice presidents and Cabinet members are empowered by the Twenty-fifth Amendment to make a determination of disability. Historically, vice presidents have behaved very cautiously during presidential illnesses. They are subject to impeachment if they attempt to usurp the presidency. President Wilson's wife and doctors did conceal his stroke from the public, leaving the vice president and Cabinet in the dark (see Chapter 7), but that was before the Twenty-fifth Amendment was passed. More recently, after a presidential assassination attempt, members of the White House staff made the questionable determination that President Reagan was not disabled, and the vice president and Cabinet went along with their judgment. Luckily that judgment was not tested by a foreign or domestic crisis. The 1988 Miller Commission guidelines offered a number of recommendations to clarify provisions of the Twenty-fifth Amendment regarding presidential disability, including suggestions that the White House staff should not govern by itself and should deal honestly with the public, and that the White House physician should be consulted regularly on the state of the president's health. Of course, additional safeguards could also produce unanticipated consequences, much as the Twenty-fifth Amendment did when it was first invoked in 1974.

Despite its demonstrated flaws and the failure to agree on reforms to correct them, the vice presidency has come a long way. No longer can a vice president draw a self-portrait in the fashion of Vice President Marshall, who characterized himself as "a man in a cataleptic state; he cannot speak; he cannot move; he suffers no pain; and yet he is perfectly conscious of everything that is going on about him."[20] It is time for Americans to reappraise and reevaluate their vice presidents, giving credit to these presidential understudies for the work they do while waiting in the wings, readying themselves, if called on, to take over from the nation's leader.

NOTES

CHAPTER ONE

1. Sol Barzman, *Madmen and Geniuses: The Vice-Presidents of the United States* (Chicago: Follett Publishing Co., 1974), p. 312.
2. Michael Nelson, *A Heartbeat Away: Report of the Twentieth Century Fund Task Force on the Vice Presidency* (New York: Priority Press, 1988), pp. 31–34.
3. Edgar Waugh, *Second Consul: The Vice-Presidency: Our Greatest Political Problem* (Indianapolis: Bobbs-Merrill Company, 1956), p. 38.
4. Barzman, p. 249.
5. Irving G. Williams, *The Rise of the Vice Presidency* (Washington, D.C.: Public Affairs Press, 1956), p. 252.
6. Nelson, p. 6.
7. Ibid., p. 33.
8. *World Almanac and Books of Facts 1994* (Mahwah, N.J.: Funk & Wagnalls, 1994), p. 81.
9. Waugh, pp. 55–56.

CHAPTER TWO

1. John D. Feerick, *From Failing Hands: The Story of Presidential Succession* (New York: Fordham University Press, 1965), p. 43.

2. Arthur M. Schlesinger, Jr., "The Future of the Vice Presidency," *The Cycles of American History* (Boston: Houghton Mifflin Co., 1986), p. 339.

3 Max Farrand, ed., *The Records of the Federal Convention of 1787*, 4 vols. (New Haven: Yale University Press, 1911), vol. 2, p. 499.

4. Ibid., p. 537.

5. Ibid., p. 536–37.

6. Ibid., p. 537.

7. Ibid., p. 537.

8. Ibid., p. 535.

9. Sidney M. Miklis and Michael Nelson, *The American Presidency: Origins and Development, 1776-1990* (Washington, D.C.: Congressional Quarterly Press, 1990), p. 56.

10. Feerick, pp. 48–51.

11. Ibid., p. 53.

12. Ibid.

13. Ibid., p. 54.

14. Alexander Hamilton, John Jay, and James Madison, *The Federalist* (New York: Modern Library, n.d.), pp. 444–45.

15. Edgar Waugh, *Second Consul: The Vice-Presidency: Our Greatest Political Problem* (Indianapolis: Bobbs-Merrill Co., 1956), p. 28.

16. Alvin M. Josephy, Jr., *On the Hill: A History of the American Congress* (New York: Simon & Schuster, 1979), p. 44.

17. Ibid., p. 42.

18. Ibid. p. 45.

19. Miklis, p. 73.

20. Charles F. Adams, ed., *The Works of John Adams*, 10 vols. (Boston: Little, Brown, 1850–56), vol. 1, p. 460.

21. Josephy, p. 46.

22. 5 U.S. Code 16 (1958).

23. Waugh, p. 35.

24. Ibid., p. 36.

25. Ibid.

26. Irving G.Williams, *The Rise of the Vice Presidency* (Washington, D.C.: Public Affairs Press, 1956), p. 22.

27. Adams, vol. 1, p. 289.

CHAPTER THREE

1. Paul F. Boller, Jr., *Presidential Campaigns* (New York: Oxford University Press, 1984), p. 15.
2. Charles C. Euchner and John Anthony Maltese. *Selecting the President* (Washington, D.C.: Congressional Quarterly, 1992), p. 183.
3. Jules Witcover, *Crapshoot: Rolling the Dice on the Vice Presidency* (New York: Crown Publishers, 1992), p. 23.
4. John D. Feerick, *From Failing Hands: The Story of Presidential Succession* (New York: Fordham University Press, 1965), pp. 73–74.
5. Ibid., p. 74.
6. Barbara Silberdick Feinberg, *American Political Scandals Past and Present* (New York: Franklin Watts, 1992), pp. 54–55.
7. Sidney M. Miklis and Michael Nelson, *The American Presidency: Origins and Development, 1776–1990* (Washington, D.C.: Congressional Quarterly Press, 1990), p. 360.
8. Sol Barzman, *Madmen and Geniuses: The Vice-Presidents of the United States* (Chicago: Follett Publishing Co., 1974), p. 38.
9. Steve Tally, *Bland Ambition* (San Diego: Harcourt Brace Jovanovich, 1992), p.154.
10. Ibid., p. 201.
11. Ibid., p. 202.
12. Barzman, p. 171.
13. Witcover, pp. 152–53, 158; see Chapter 6.
14. Diana Dixon Healy, *America's Vice-Presidents: Our First Forty-three Vice-Presidents and How They Got to Be Number Two* (New York: Atheneum, 1984), p. 234.
15. Tally, p. 396.
16. Ibid., p. 398.
17. For a discussion of the Eagelton candidacy, see Feinberg, pp. 99–102.
18. John D. Feerick, *The Twenty-Fifth Amendment: Its Complete History and Applications* (New York: Fordham University Press, 1992), Appendix D II.
19. Ibid., p. 66.
20. Witcover, p. 265.

21. Ibid., p. 266.
22. Feerick, *The Twenty-Fifth Amendment*, p. 136.
23. Barzman, p. 300.
24. Ibid.
25. Ibid.
26. Joel K. Goldstein, *The Modern American Vice Presidency: The Transformation of a Political Institution* (Princeton: Princeton University Press, 1984), p. 245.
27. Feerick, *The Twenty-Fifth Amendment*, p. 184.

CHAPTER FOUR

1. Steve Tally, *Bland Ambition* (San Diego: Harcourt Brace Jovanovich, 1992), p. 28.
2. Ibid., p. 25.
3. Ibid., p. 28.
4. John C. Breckinridge, President James Buchanan's vice president from 1857 to 1861, was also accused of treason, the charges stemming from his service as a Confederate general during the Civil War and briefly as Jefferson Davis's secretary of war in 1865. After the war, he lived abroad until President Andrew Johnson issued a general amnesty in 1868 which allowed him to return home without having to face the possibility of imprisonment. The charges against him, however, were not dismissed until 1958.
5. Irving G. Williams, *The Rise of the Vice Presidency* (Washington, D.C.: Public Affairs Press, 1956), p. 36.
6. Sol Barzman, *Madmen and Geniuses: The Vice-Presidents of the United States* (Chicago: Follett Publishing Co., 1974), p. 49.
7. Diana Dixon Healy, *America's Vice-Presidents: Our First Forty-three Vice-Presidents and How They Got to Be Number Two* (New York: Atheneum, 1984), p. 36.
8. Williams, p. 37.
9. Barzman, p. 50.
10. Edgar Waugh, *Second Consul: The Vice-Presidency: Our Greatest Political Problem* (Indianapolis: Bobbs-Merrill Company, 1956), p. 76.
11. Ibid., pp. 77–78.
12. Tally, p. 136.
13. Barzman, p. 124.

14. Ibid.
15. Tally, pp. 299–300.
16. Jules Witcover, *Crapshoot: Rolling the Dice on the Vice Presidency* (New York: Crown Publishers, 1992), p. 114.
17. Ibid., p. 116.
18. Tally, p. 302.
19. Witcover, p. 119.
20. Ibid., p. 120.
21. Ibid., p. 121.
22. Barbara Silberdick Feinberg, *American Political Scandals Past and Present* (New York: Franklin Watts, 1992), p. 79.
23. Merle Miller, *Lyndon: An Oral Biography* (New York: Putnam, 1980), p. 298.
24. Donald Young, *American Roulette: The History and Dilemma of the Vice Presidency* (New York: Holt, Rinehart & Winston, 1972), p. 348.
25. Tally, p. 342.
26. Barzman, p. 291.
27. Tally, p. 342.

CHAPTER FIVE

1. Irving G. Williams, *The Rise of the Vice Presidency* (Washington, D.C.: Public Affairs Press, 1956), p. 25.
2. Charles F. Adams, ed., *The Works of John Adams*, 10 vols. (Boston: Little, Brown, 1850–56), vol. 2, p. 98.
3. Joel K. Goldstein, *The Modern American Vice Presidency: The Transformation of a Political Institution* (Princeton: Princeton University Press, 1984), p. 137.
4. Steve Tally, *Bland Ambition* (San Diego: Harcourt Brace Jovanovich, 1992), p. 15.
5. John D. Feerick, *From Failing Hands: The Story of Presidential Succession* (New York: Fordham University Press, 1965), p. 71.
6. Diana Dixon Healy, *America's Vice-Presidents: Our First Forty-three Vice-Presidents and How They Got to Be Number Two* (New York: Atheneum, 1984), p. 18.
7. Donald Young, *American Roulette: The History and Dilemma of the Vice Presidency* (New York: Holt, Rinehart & Winston, 1972), p.18.

8. Alvin M. Josephy, Jr., *On the Hill: A History of the American Congress* (New York: Simon & Schuster, 1979), p. 126.
9. Young, p. 19.
10. Healy, p. 25.
11. John Niven, *John C. Calhoun and the Price of Union* (Baton Rouge: Louisiana State University Press, 1988), p. 109.
12. Williams, p. 39.
13. Niven, p. 173.
14. Young, p. 32.
15. Sol Barzman, *Madmen and Geniuses: The Vice-Presidents of the United States* (Chicago: Follett Publishing Co., 1974), p. 64.
16. Healy, p. 42.
17. Williams, p. 90.
18. Healy, p. 146.
19. Williams, p. 94.
20. Young, pp. 123–24.
21. Barzman, p. 134.
22. Young, p. 157.
23. Barzman, p. 210.
24. Williams, p. 138.
25. Ibid.
26. Ibid., p. 164.
27. Ibid., p. 163.
28. Ibid., p. 164.
29. Barzman, p. 226.
30. Young, p. 170.
31. Ibid., p. 171.
32. Williams, p. 173.

CHAPTER SIX

1. See John D. Feerick, From Failing Hands: *The Story of Presidential Succession* (New York: Fordham University Press, 1965), pp. 48–51 and Chapter 2 for a discussion of the founders' intentions and how the Committee on Style inadvertently changed the wording of the succession clause. For a more detailed examination of nine vice presidents who succeeded to the presidency, see Edmund Lindop, *Presidents by Accident* (New York: Franklin Watts, 1991).

2. Donald Young, *American Roulette: The History and Dilemma of the Vice Presidency* (New York: Holt, Rinehart & Winston, 1972), p. 45.
3. Edgar Waugh, *Second Consul: The Vice-Presidency: Our Greatest Political Problem* (Indianapolis: Bobbs-Merrill Company, 1956), p. 71.
4. Ibid., p. 72.
5. See Chapter 2, and Waugh, p. 73.
6. Diana Dixon Healy, *America's Vice-Presidents: Our First Forty-three Vice-Presidents and How They Got to Be Number Two* (New York: Atheneum, 1984), p. 55.
7. Young, p. 49.
8. Ibid.
9. Irving G. Williams, *The Rise of the Vice Presidency* (Washington, D.C.: Public Affairs Press, 1956), p. 46.
10. Ibid., p. 55.
11. Young, p. 61.
12. Ibid., p. 81.
13. For a detailed acount of the issues and proceedings see Waugh, pp. 102–20.
14. Sol Barzman, *Madmen and Geniuses: The Vice-Presidents of the United States* (Chicago: Follett Publishing Co., 1974), p. 137.
15. Williams, p. 66.
16. Steve Tally, *Bland Ambition* (San Diego: Harcourt Brace Jovanovich, 1992), p. 165.
17. Tally, p. 204, See Chapter 3.
18. Feerick, p. 158.
19. Young, p. 120.
20. Barzman, p. 124.
21. Irving Stone, "Calvin Coolidge: A Study in Inertia," *The Aspirin Age 1919–1941*, ed. Isabel Leighton (New York: Simon & Schuster, 1949), p. 144.
22. Jules Witcover, *Crapshoot: Rolling the Dice on the Vice-Presidency* (New York: Crown Publishers, 1992) p. 66.
23. Williams, p. 126.
24. Young, p. 151.
25. Ibid., p. 152.
26. John D. Feerick, *The Twenty-Fifth Amendment: Its Complete History and Applications* (New York: Fordham University Press, 1992), pp. 15–16.

181

27. David McCullough, *Truman* (New York: Simon & Schuster, 1992), p. 348.
28. Ibid., p. 353.
29. Harry S. Truman, *Year of Decisions* (Garden City: Doubleday & Co., 1955), p. 53.
30. Tally, p. 319.
31. Ibid.
32. Witcover, p. 166.
33. Merle Miller, *Lyndon: An Oral Biography* (New York: Putnam, 1980), p. 322.
34. Ibid., p. 330.
35. Witcover, p. 173.
36. Tally, p. 349.
37. Feerick, pp. 156–57.
38. Marie D. Natoli, *American Prince, American Pauper: The Contemporary Vice Presidency in Perspective* (Westport, Conn.: Greenwood Press, 1985), p. 86.
39. William A. De Gregorio, *The Complete Book of U.S. Presidents*, 4th ed. (New York: Barricade Books, 1993), p. 612.

CHAPTER SEVEN

1. Virginia Moore, *The Madisons: A Biography* (New York: McGraw-Hill, 1979), p. 290.
2. John D. Feerick, *The Twenty-Fifth Amendment: Its Complete History and Applications* (New York: Fordham University Press, 1992), p. 9.
3. In 1792, Congress made the President Pro Tempore and the Speaker of the House the successors to the presidency in the event that both the president and vice president could not complete their terms. In 1886, after the death of Vice President Thomas A. Hendricks, Congress decided to revise the succession law so that a Cabinet officer, starting with the secretary of state, rather than a presiding officer of Congress, would become the replacement president if the vice president could not. [John D. Feerick, *From Failing Hands: The Story of Presidential Succession* (New York: Fordham University Press, 1965), pp. 141–43.] At the time of Garfield's and Hendrick's deaths, the office of President Pro Tempore of the

Senate and Speaker of the House, successors under the 1792 law, were vacant.

In 1947, Congress decided that elective officers should succeed the president and vice president and made the Speaker of the House and the President Pro Tempore of the Senate their heirs so that the president would not be in a position to name a possible successor, for example, the secretary of state. The Speaker was given preference over the President Pro Tempore because the speaker would have been elected more recently. Members of the House serve two-year terms while senators serve six.

4. Feerick, *The Twenty-Fifth Amendment*, p. 12.
5. Thomas R. Marshall, *Recollections of Thomas R. Marshall: Vice-President and Hoosier Philosopher*, (Indianapolis: Bobbs-Merrill, 1925), p. 368.
6. Irving G. Williams, *The Rise of the Vice Presidency* (Washington, D.C.: Public Affairs Press, 1956), p. 101.
7. Feerick, *From Failing Hands*, p. 173.
8. Donald Young, *American Roulette: The History and Dilemma of the Vice Presidency* (New York: Holt, Rinehart & Winston, 1972), p. 137.
9. Feerick, *From Failing Hands*, p. 172.
10. Ibid., p. 176.
11. Sol Barzman, *Madmen and Geniuses: The Vice-Presidents of the United States* (Chicago: Follett Publishing Co., 1974), p. 194.
12. Ibid.
13. Feerick, *From Failing Hands*, p. 175.
14. Marshall, p. 17.
15. Jules Witcover, *Crapshoot: Rolling the Dice on the Vice Presidency* (New York: Crown Publishers, 1992), p. 126.
16. Feerick, *The Twenty-Fifth Amendment*, p. 18.
17. Witcover, p. 127.
18. Feerick, *From Failing Hands*, note bottom p. 218.
19. Witcover, pp. 127–28; also see Marie D. Natoli, *American Prince, American Pauper: The Contemporary Vice Presidency in Perspective* (Westport, Conn.: Greenwood Press, 1985), p. 94.

20. Young, p. 266.
21. Feerick, *The Twenty-Fifth Amendment*, p. 20.
22. Ibid., p. 21.
23. This paragraph is a synopsis of Feerick, *The Twenty-Fifth Amendment*, pp. 55–56.
24. Richard B. Bernstein and Jerome Agel, *Amending America* (New York: Random House-Times Books, 1993), p. 164.
25. Ibid., p. 165; Young, pp. 395–96; Natoli, pp. 90–91.
26. Witcover, p. 318.
27. Feerick, *The Twenty-Fifth Amendment*, p. xiv.
28. Ibid.
29. Ibid., p. 25 xv.
30. Ibid.
31. Ibid., pp. xvi-xvii.
32. For more specifics see Ibid., p. xxi.

CHAPTER EIGHT

1. John D. Feerick, *From Failing Hands: The Story of Presidential Succession* (New York: Fordham University Press, 1965), p. 100.
2. Ibid.
3. Irving G. Williams, *The Rise of the Vice Presidency* (Washington, D.C.: Public Affairs Press, 1956), p. 7.
4. Diana Dixon Healy, *America's Vice-Presidents: Our First Forty-three Vice-Presidents and How They Got to Be Number Two* (New York: Atheneum, 1984), p. 173.
5. Paul C. Light, *Vice-Presidential Power: Advice and Influence in the White House* (Baltimore: Johns Hopkins University Press, 1984), pp. 53–54.
6. Marie D. Natoli, *American Prince, American Pauper: The Contemporary Vice Presidency in Perspective* (Westport, Conn.: Greenwood Press, 1985), p. 11.
7. Steve Tally, *Bland Ambition* (San Diego: Harcourt Brace Jovanovich, 1992), p. 293.
8. Light, p. 38.
9. Tally, p. 308.
10. Jules Witcover, *Crapshoot: Rolling the Dice on the Vice Presidency* (New York: Crown Publishers, 1992), p. 136.
11. Healy, p. 205.
12. Natoli, p. 10.

13. Ibid., p. 150.
14. Witcover, p. 227.
15. Natoli, p. 155.
16. Ibid., p. 152.
17. Witcover, pp. 222–23.
18. Natoli, pp. 8–9.
19. Witcover, p. 280.
20. Joel K. Goldstein, *The Modern American Vice Presidency: The Transformation of a Political Institution* (Princeton: Princeton University Press, 1984), p. 309.
21. Ibid., pp. 172–73.
22. Light, p. 47.
23. Arthur M. Schlesinger, Jr., "The Future of the Vice Presidency," *The Cycles of American History* (Boston: Houghton Mifflin Co., 1986), p. 359.
24. Goldstein, p. 159.
25. Light, p. 37.
26. Natoli, p.181.
27. Witcover, p. 395.
28. Michael Duffy, "Is He Really That Bad?" *Time*, vol. 137, May 20, 1991, p. 22.
29. Witcover, p. 389.
30. Peter J. Boyer, "The Political Scene: Gore's Dilemma," *The New Yorker*, LXX, 39 (November 28, 1994), p. 110.

CHAPTER NINE

1. Arthur M. Schlesinger, Jr., "The Future of the Vice Presidency," *The Cycles of American History* (Boston: Houghton Mifflin Co., 1986), p. 341.
2. Ibid., p. 367.
3. Edgar Waugh, *Second Consul: The Vice-Presidency: Our Greatest Political Problem* (Indianapolis: Bobbs-Merrill Company, 1956), p. 169.
4. Joel K. Goldstein, *The Modern American Vice Presidency: The Transformation of a Political Institution* (Princeton: Princeton University Press, 1984), p. 142.
5. Waugh, pp. 167–68.
6. Donald Young, *American Roulette: The History and Dilemma of the Vice Presidency* (New York: Holt, Rinehart & Winston, 1972), p. 179.
7. Schlesinger, pp. 370–71.

8. Ibid., p. 361.
9. Ibid., p. 363.
10. Ibid. p. 360.
11. Waugh, pp. 180–81.
12. Marie D. Natoli, *American Prince, American Pauper: The Contemporary Vice Presidency in Perspective* (Westport, Conn.: Greenwood Press, 1985), p. 183.
13. Jules Witcover, *Crapshoot: Rolling the Dice on the Vice Presidency* (New York: Crown Publishers, 1992), p. 405.
14. Young, p. 381.
15. Michael Nelson, *A Heartbeat Away: Report of the Twentieth Century Fund Task Force on the Vice Presidency* (New York: Priority Press, 1988), p. 12.
16. Ibid., pp. 51-52.
17. Natoli, p. 91.
18. John D. Feerick, *The Twenty-Fifth Amendment: Its Complete History and Applications* (New York: Fordham University Press, 1992), p. 233.
19. Schlesinger, p. 353.
20. Diana Dixon Healy, *America's Vice-Presidents: Our First Forty-three Vice-Presidents and How They Got to Be Number Two* (New York: Atheneum, 1984), p. 151.

GLOSSARY

Amendment A change in the wording of the Constitution, which is proposed by two-thirds of the members of Congress and must be approved by three-fourths of the states.

Anarchist A person who does not believe in any government or law.

Balanced ticket The effort to select presidential and vice presidential candidates from different parts of the country, or holding different views, in order to appeal to the greatest number of voters nationwide.

Brokered conventions Where political bosses in "smoke-filled rooms" choose the party's candidates for president and vice president because they control state delegations.

Cabinet The heads of government departments and other officials, such as the vice president, who advise the president.

Cloture A vote to shut off unlimited debate in the Senate.

Deficit spending An economic practice, which lets the government spend more money than it takes in from taxes and fees.

187

Electoral college A method of electing the president and vice president of the United States. Since passage of the Twelfth Amendment, electors, chosen by each state and determined by its number of senators and representatives, cast separate ballots for the presidential and vice presidential candidates who have won the state's popular vote. In Maine and Nebraska, however, electoral votes are distributed in proportion to the popular vote, so the losers of the popular election receive a percentage of the votes.

Extradition The transfer of a prisoner or a fugitive from justice from one state or nation to another upon request.

Filibuster The Senate tradition of unlimited free speech that can result in talking marathons to defeat proposed laws.

Gerrymandering A process of partisan redistricting, allowing the boundaries of election districts to be readjusted in favor of the political party in power, resulting in some oddly shaped, unequal, and biased voting divisions.

Impeachment A legislative process used to remove officials from office. On the federal level, the House of Representatives may decide to bring charges against an office holder, and the Senate holds a trial to determine guilt or innocence.

Incumbent The person who holds an elective or an appointive office until replaced by a challenger or a successor.

Indictment Formal accusations, or charges, that a person has committed a crime.

Lame duck Term used to describe an official who will be leaving office but continues to serve out the remainder of an elected term.

Majority leader A powerful lawmaker from the majority party in Congress who helps determine committee assignments for members of the party and the items to be taken up for debate and vote.

Patronage The distribution of political jobs, usually by means of appointment.

Platform A statement of campaign promises for specific programs or positions with which a political party is prepared to be associated.

Political bosses Leaders who controlled a bloc of delegates and their votes. The bosses' power was based in state or local government, where they exchanged jobs, contracts for public works, and other services or favors for votes they could count on in elections to party organizations and to government.

President pro tempore The presiding officer of the Senate, in the absence of the vice president, who is chosen from among the senators of the majority party.

Ratification A formal process of granting approval; in the case of constitutional amendments, ratification requires a favorable vote in three-fourths of the states.

Separation of powers The constitutional principle that divides the government of the United States into three distinct branches: the legislative, executive, and judicial, to make, carry out, and interpret law.

Tariff Fees charged on goods imported for sale in the United States.

Veto The president's power to prevent a bill from becoming law by refusing to sign it.

BIBLIOGRAPHY

* Books especially recommended for students

Adams, Charles F., ed. *The Works of John Adams*. 10 vols. Boston: Little, Brown, 1850–56.

*Barzman, Sol. *Madmen and Geniuses: The Vice-Presidents of the United States*. Chicago: Follett Publishing Co., 1974.

Berke, Richard L. "Al Gore: The Good Scout." *New York Times Magazine*, February 20, 1994, pp. 28–35, 44, 54, 57, 62.

Bernstein, Richard B. and Jerome Agel. *Amending America*. New York: Random House–Times Books, 1993.

Boller, Paul F., Jr. *Presidential Campaigns*. New York: Oxford University Press, 1984.

Boyer, Peter J. "The Political Scene: Gore's Dilemma." *The New Yorker*, LXX, 39, November 28, 1994, pp. 100–10.

De Gregorio, William A. *The Complete Book of U.S. Presidents*. 4th ed. New York: Barricade Books, 1993.

Duffy, Michael. "Is He Really That Bad?" *Time*, vol. 137, May 20, 1991, pp. 21–22.

Euchner, Charles C., and John Anthony Maltese. *Selecting the President*. Washington, D.C.: Congressional Quarterly, 1992.

Farrand, Max, ed. *The Records of the Federal Convention of 1787*. 4 vols. New Haven: Yale University Press, 1911, vol. 2.

Feerick, John D. *From Failing Hands: The Story of Presidential Succession*. New York: Fordham University Press, 1965.

_____. *The Twenty-Fifth Amendment: Its Complete History and Applications*. New York: Fordham University Press, 1992.

*Feinberg, Barbara Silberdick. *American Political Scandals Past and Present*. New York: Franklin Watts, 1992.

Goldstein, Joel K. *The Modern American Vice Presidency: The Transformation of a Political Institution*. Princeton: Princeton University Press, 1984.

Hamilton, Alexander, John Jay, and James Madison. *The Federalist*. New York: The Modern Library, n.d., pp. 441–45.

*Healy, Diana Dixon. *America's Vice-Presidents: Our First Forty-three Vice-Presidents and How They Got to Be Number Two*. New York: Atheneum, 1984.

Josephy, Alvin M., Jr. *On the Hill: A History of the American Congress*. New York: Simon & Schuster, 1979.

Light, Paul C. *Vice-Presidential Power: Advice and Influence in the White House*. Baltimore: Johns Hopkins University Press, 1984.

*Lindop, Edmund. *Presidents by Accident.* New York: Franklin Watts, 1991.

Madison, James. "Reports on the Debates in the Federal Convention." *The Papers of James Madison.* 3 vols. Washington, D.C.: Langtree and O'Sullivan, 1840, vol. 3.

Marshall, Thomas R. *Recollections of Thomas R. Marshall: Vice-President and Hoosier Philosopher.* Indianapolis: Bobbs-Merrill Co., 1925.

McCullough, David. *Truman.* New York: Simon & Schuster, 1992.

Milkis, Sidney M. and Michael Nelson. *The American Presidency: Origins and Development, 1776–1990.* Washington, D.C.: Congressional Quarterly Press, 1990, pp. 54–57, 357–75.

Miller, Merle. *Lyndon: An Oral Biography.* New York: Putnam, 1980.

Moore, Virginia. *The Madisons: A Biography.* New York: McGraw-Hill, 1979.

Natoli, Marie D. *American Prince, American Pauper: The Contemporary Vice Presidency in Perspective.* Westport, Conn.: Greenwood Press, 1985.

Nelson, Michael. *A Heartbeat Away: Report of the Twentieth Century Fund Task Force on the Vice Presidency.* New York: Priority Press, 1988.

Niven, John. *John C. Calhoun and the Price of Union.* Baton Rouge: Louisiana State University Press, 1988.

Schlesinger, Arthur M., Jr. "The Future of the Vice Presidency." *The Cycles of American History.* Boston: Houghton Mifflin Co., 1986, pp. 337–72.

Sciolino, Elaine, and Todd S. Purdum. "Al Gore, One Vice President Who Is Eluding the Shadows," *New York Times*, February 19, 1995, sec. 1, pp. 1, 32.

Stone, Irving. "Calvin Coolidge: A Study in Inertia." *The Aspirin Age 1919–1941*, ed. Isabel Leighton. New York: Simon & Schuster, 1949, pp. 130–51.

*Tally, Steve. *Bland Ambition.* San Diego: Harcourt Brace Jovanovich, 1992.

Truman, Harry S. *Year of Decisions.* Garden City: Doubleday, 1955.

Waugh, Edgar. *Second Consul: The Vice-Presidency: Our Greatest Political Problem.* Indianapolis: Bobbs-Merrill Co., 1956.

Williams, Irving G. *The Rise of the Vice Presidency.* Washington, D.C.: Public Affairs Press, 1956.

Witcover, Jules. *Crapshoot: Rolling the Dice on the Vice Presidency.* New York: Crown Publishers, 1992.

Woodward, Bob. *The Agenda: Inside The Clinton White House.* New York: Pocket Books, 1995.

World Almanac and Books of Facts 1995. Mahwah, N.J.: Funk & Wagnalls, 1995.

Young, Donald. *American Roulette: The History and Dilemma of the Vice Presidency.* New York: Holt, Rinehart & Winston, 1972.

Young, Klyde, and Kamar Middleton. *Heirs Apparent: The Vice Presidents of the United States.* New York: Prentice-Hall, 1948.

APPENDIX

*	Died in office
**	Resigned
***	President by succession
G	Former governor
H	Former member of the House of Repreentatives
S	Former United States senator
O	Other service in government

VICE PRESIDENTS	HOME	TERM
John Adams (1735–1826)	Massachusetts	1789–1793 1793–1797
Thomas Jefferson (1743–1826)	Virginia	1787–1801
Aaron Burr (1756–1836)	New York	1801–1805
George Clinton* (1739–1812)	New York	1805–1809 1809–1812
Elbridge Gerry* (1744–1814)	Massachusetts	1813–1814
Daniel D. Tompkins (1774–1825)	New York	1817–1821 1821–1825
John C. Calhoun** (1782–1850)	S. Carolina	1825–1829 1829–1832
Martin Van Buren (1782–1862)	New York	1833–1836
Richard M. Johnson (1780–1850)	Kentucky	1837–1841

PRESIDENT	PARTY	EXPERIENCE
George Washington	Federalist	O
George Washington	Federalist	
John Adams	Democratic-Republican	G,O
Thomas Jefferson	Democratic-Republican	S
Thomas Jefferson	Democratic-Republican	G
James Madison	Democratic-Republican	G
James Madison	Democratic-Republican	
James Monroe	Democratic-Republican	G,H
James Monroe	Democratic-Republican	
John Quincy Adams	Democratic-Republican	H
Andrew Jackson	Democratic-Republican	
Andrew Jackson	Democrat	G,S
Martin Van Buren	Democrat	H,S

VICE PRESIDENTS	HOME	TERM
John Tyler*** (1790–1862)	Virginia	1841
George M. Dallas (1792–1864)	Pennsylvania	1845–1849
Millard Fillmore*** (1800–1874)	New York	1849–1850
William R. DeVane King* (1786–1853)	Alabama	1853
John C. Breckinridge (1821–1875)	Kentucky	1857–1861
Hannibal Hamlin (1809–1891)	Maine	1861–1865
Andrew Johnson*** (1808–1875)	Tennessee	1865
Schuyler Colfax (1823–1885)	Indiana	1869–1873
Henry Wilson* (1812–1875)	Massachusetts	1873–1875
William Wheeler (1819–1887)	New York	1877–1881
Chester A. Arthur*** (1829–1886)	New York	1881
Thomas A. Hendricks* (1819–1885)	Indiana	1885

PRESIDENT	PARTY	EXPERIENCE
William H. Harrison	Whig	G, H, S
James Polk	Democrat	S
Zachary Taylor	Whig	H
Franklin Pierce	Democrat	H, S
James Buchanan	Democrat	H
Abraham Lincoln	Republican	G, H, S
Abraham Lincoln	National Union	G, H, S
Ulysses S. Grant	Republican	H
Ulysses S. Grant	Republican	S
Rutherford B. Hayes	Republican	H
James Garfield	Republican	O
Grover Cleveland	Democrat	G, H, S

VICE PRESIDENTS	HOME	TERM
Levi P. Morton (1824–1920)	New York	1889–1893
Adlai E. Stevenson (1835–1914)	Illinois	1893–1897
Garret A. Hobart* (1844–1899)	New Jersey	1897–1899
Theodore Roosevelt*** (1858–1919)	New York	1901
Charles W. Fairbanks (1852–1918)	Indiana	1905–1909
James S. Sherman* (1855–1912)	New York	1909–1912
Thomas R. Marshall (1854–1925)	Indiana	1913–1921
Calvin Coolidge*** (1872–1933)	Massachusetts	1921–1923
Charles G. Dawes (1865–1951)	Illinois	1925–1929
Charles Curtis (1860–1936)	Kansas	1929–1933
John Nance Garner (1868–1967)	Texas	1933–1941
Henry A. Wallace (1888–1965)	Iowa	1941–1945

PRESIDENT	PARTY	EXPERIENCE
Benjamin Harison	Republican	H
Grover Cleveland	Democrat	H
William McKinley	Republican	O
William McKinley	Republican	G
Theodore Roosevelt	Republican	S
William H. Taft	Republican	H
Woodrow Wilson	Democrat	G
Warren G. Harding	Republican	G
Calvin Coolidge	Republican	O
Herbert C. Hoover	Republican	H, S
Franklin D. Roosevelt	Democrat	H
Franklin D. Roosevelt	Democrat	O

199

VICE PRESIDENTS	HOME	TERM
Harry S. Truman*** (1884–1972)	Missouri	1945
Alben W. Barkley (1877–1956)	Kentucky	1949–1953
Richard M. Nixon (1913–1994)	California	1953–1961
Lyndon B. Johnson*** (1908-1973)	Texas	1961–1963
Hubert H. Humphrey (1911–1978)	Minnesota	1965–1969
Spiro T. Agnew** (1918–)	Maryland	1969–1973
Gerald R. Ford*** (1913–)	Michigan	1973–1974
Nelson A. Rockefeller (1908–1979)	New York	1974–1977
Walter F. Mondale (1928–)	Minnesota	1977–1981
George Bush (1924–)	Texas	1981–1989
J. Danforth Quayle (1947–)	Indiana	1989–1993
Albert A. Gore, Jr. (1948–)	Tennessee	1993–

PRESIDENT	PARTY	EXPERIENCE
Franklin D. Roosevelt	Democrat	S
Harry S. Truman	Democrat	H, S
Dwight D. Eisenhower	Republican	H, S
John F. Kennedy	Democrat	H, S
Lyndon B. Johnson	Democrat	S
Richard M. Nixon	Republican	G
Richard M. Nixon	Republican	H
Gerald R. Ford	Republican	G, O
Jimmy Carter	Democrat	S
Ronald W. Reagan	Republican	H, O
George Bush	Republican	H, S
Bill Clinton	Democrat	H, S

INDEX

Adams, John, 10, 12, 15, 20, 28–33, *29*, 34, 35, 36, 43, 73–75, 77, 145

Adams, John Quincy, 34, 59, 79–81, 97

Agnew, Spiro T., 10, 17, 50, 55, 69–71, *71*, 85, 117, 152–53, 155, 158, 160

Alabama, 155

Alaska, 109

Allen, James, 155

Allen, William, 97

Ames, Oakes, 64

Arkansas, 46, 160

Arthur, Chester Alan, 11, 34, 43, 95, 104–107, 121, 122–23, 165

Baker, Robert G. "Bobby," 68–69

Barkley, Alben W., 12, 93, 139, 147–49

Bayard, James, 37

Bayh, Birch, 49, 133

Benton, Thomas Hart, 84

Bentsen, Lloyd, 47–48

Blaine, James G., 106, 122

Burger, Warren, 51, *52*, 53, 118

Burr, Aaron, 34, 35, 37, 38, 43, 54, 55–57, *57*, 73, 75–77

Bush, George, 10, 13, 15, 17, 46, *47*, 52, 134–38, *135*, 139, 141, 158–59

Caldwell, David, 26

Calhoun, Floride, 81

Calhoun, John C., 10, 17, 34, 73, 79–85, *83*, 99

California, 51, 65, 99, 100

Callender, James T., 75

Carter, Jimmy, 45, 48, 156, 160

Chase, Salmon P., 102, 103

Chase, Samuel, 77

Chinn, Julia, 61

Christopher, Warren, 162

Civil rights, 115, 150, 153

Civil War, 101, 143

Clay, Henry, 80, 97, 98, 99, 100

Cleveland, Grover, 43, 45, 85, 120, 123–24

Clinton, Bill, 46, 160, 161, *162*
Clinton, De Witt, 58
Clinton, George, 10, 26, 32, 39, 58, 73, 77–79, *78*
Colbath, Jeremiah J. *See* Henry Wilson
Colfax, Schuyler, 9, 54, 63–64
Committee on Postponed Matters, 23, 24, 25
Compromise of 1850, 99–101
Congress, U.S., 15, 21, 22, 25, 30, 31, 36, 49, 50, 51, 64, 65, 70, 73, 84, 86 92, 97, 98, 102, 114, 115, 117, 119, 121, 123, 127, 129, 132, 133, 136, 143, 144, 147, 148, 149, 150, 152, 154, 160, 162, 165, 167, 168, 169, 171, 173. *See also* House of Representatives, Senate
Conkling, Roscoe, 43, 104, 105, 107
Connally, John, 51
Connecticut, 21, 30, 97, 165, 166
Constitution, U.S., 18, 20–27, 30, 32, 34, 35, 38, 49, 57, 73, 75, 79, 84, 96, 97, 105, 120, 122, 167, 170. *See also* specific amendments
Constitutional Convention, 10, 20–27, *22*
Coolidge, Calvin, 11, 42, 86–90, 95, 109–11, *111*, 145, 150, 165, 166
Cranch, William, 96, 100
Curtis, Charles G., 15, 44

Dallas, George M., 9, 139, 141–42, 150
Dana, Samuel W., 165, 166

Daniels, Josephus, 126
Dawes, Charles G., 17, 42, 73, 86–90, *88*, 165, 167
Dayton, Jonathan, 165, 166
Delaware, 37, 38
Democratic party, 40, 44, 45, 46, 47, 48, 50, 61, 65, 79, 82, 85, 89, 92, 96, 97, 102, 111, 112, 114, 117, 124, 130, 132, 133, 140, 144, 147, 149, 156, 160
Democratic-Republican party, 35, 36, 37, 58, 59, 73, 74, 76, 77
Dole, Bob, 156
Dulles, John Foster, 131

Eagleton, Thomas F., 48
"Eaton affair," 81–82
Eisenhower, Dwight D., 13, 45, 65, 66, 67–68, 120, 128–33, *129*, 136, 149, 168
Elections
    1789, 27–28
    1792, 31–32
    1796, 35–36, 73–74
    1800, 36–38, 76
    1824, 79–80
    1828, 81
    1832, 84
    1836, 61
    1860, 142
    1868, 63
    1884, 85
    1900, 46
    1912, 86
    1924, 111
    1936, 90
    1956, 131, 132
    1960, 132, 150
    1976, 119
    1980, 157, 158
    1992, 160

Electoral-college system, 23, 27–28, 33, 34, 36, 50, 61, 73, 79, 165
Ellsworth, Oliver, 30

Fairbanks, Charles W., 9, 42, 85
Fall, Albert B., 109
Farley, James A., 93
Federalist Paper #68 (Hamilton), 27
Federalist party, 35, 36, 37, 38, 55, 58, 73, 74, 75, 76, 77
Ferraro, Geraldine, 15–16, *18*
Fillmore, Millard, 11, 95, 99–101, *101*
Ford, Gerald, 10 13, 17, 34, 46, 51–53, *52*, 72, 95, 117–19, 154, 156, 158, 165, 169, 173
Forsyth, John, 85

Gallatin, Albert, 121, 122
Garfield, James, 34, 43, 104, 105, *106*, 122, 123, 165
Garner, John Nance, 10, 44, 63, 73, 90–93, *91*, 139, 144–45, 149, 164
Georgia, 45, 85, 156
Gerry, Elbridge, 9–10, 24, 39, 58, 75, 121
Goodall, Charles, 153
Gore, Albert, 15, 46, 139, 160–63, *162*, 164
Gorham, Nathaniel, 23
Grant, Ulysses S., 63
Griswold, Roger, 166

Haig, Alexander, 118
Half-Breed Republicans, 43, 105, 107
Hamilton, Alexander, 21–22, 27, 32, 35, 36, 37, 55–56, *57*

Hamlin, Hannibal, 62, 142, *142*, 162
Hanna, Mark, 42, 107
Harding, Warren, 109, 110
Harrison, William Henry, 44–45, 96, 97, 98
Hayes, Rutherford B., 40, 43, 104
Hayne, Robert, 82
Hazel, John R., 107
Hendricks, Thomas A., 10, 39, 43, 85
Hobart, Garret A., 10, 39, 139, 143–44, 145
Hoffman, Walter, 71
Hoover, Herbert C., 15, 44, 169
House of Representatives, U.S., 9, 12, 17, 21, 23, 26, 36, 37, 38, 39, 49, 51, 53, 55, 63, 64, 68, 79, 86, 97, 99, 103, 134, 144, 165. *See also* Congress, Senate
Houston, David, 126
Hull, Cordell, 93, 147
Humphrey, Hubert H., 10, 15, 17, 133, 139, 150–52, *151*, 157, 158, 164
Huntington, Jabez W., 97

Idaho, 153
Illinois, 43, 102
Illness. *See* Presidential disabilities and illnesses
Impeachment, 52, 63, 98, 103–104, *104*, 173
Indiana, 18, 43, 49, 90, 160
Izard, Ralph, 29
Jackson, Andrew, 39, 40, 79, 81–85, 140, 141
Jefferson, Thomas, 10, 12, 17, 30, 33, 34, 35, 36, *37*, 38, 43, 55, 56, 72, 73 76, 77

Johnson, Andrew, 11, 17, 45, 54, 61–63, 95, 102–104, *104*, 167

Johnson, Lyndon B., 13, 17, 43, *44*, 46, 49, 55, 68–69, 95, 114–17, *116*, 133, 150, *151*, 152, 158

Johnson, Richard M., 38, 54, 60–61

Johnston, Samuel, 27

Jordan, Len, 153

Kennedy, John F., 13, 16, 43, *44*, 46, 47–48, 49, 69, 114, 115, 133, 168

Kennedy, Robert, 68, 115

Kentucky, 60, 61, 97

King, William Rufus DeVane, 10–11, 39

Know-Nothing party, 101

Lamont, Daniel, 123

Lansing, Robert, 125, 127, 128, 131

League of Nations, 124, 126, 127, 128

Lee, Richard Henry, 26

Lenroot, Irvine L., 42

Lincoln, Abraham, 45, 61, 62, 102, 142, 143

Louisiana, 99

McGovern, George, 16, 47

McKinley, William, 40, 42, 47, 107, 109, 124, 143, 144

Maclay, William, 29

Madison, James, 21, 25, 27, 29, 31, 58, 74, 77, 79, 121

Maine, 98, 136, 142

Marshall, Thomas R., 9, 10, 18, 43, 74, 120, 124–28, *125*, 129, 136, 145, 167, 174

Maryland, 31, 38, 50, 69, 70, 77, 153

Mason, George, 24, 26

Massachusetts, 9, 23, 24, 28, 35, 43, 63, 97, 109, 123

Matz, Lester, 69

Michigan, 51

Miller Commission, 137, 173

Minnesota, 45, 49, 156

Mississippi, 97

Missouri, 48, 111

Mondale, Walter, 15, 45, 49, 139, 156–58, 160, 164, 166

Monroe, James, 26, 43, 46, 58, 59, 79, 84

Morris, Gouverneur, 21, 38

National Security Council, 114, 130, 131, 147, 148, 168

National Union party, 102

New Hampshire, 39, 76, 77, 82

New Jersey, 43, 55, 56, 76, 165

New Mexico, 100

New York, 17, 20, 26, 29, 37, 38, 39, 40, 43, 52, 55, 56, 57, 59, 77, 104, 105, 107, 153, 155

Nixon, Richard M., 9, 10, 12, 13, 15, 17, 45, 50, 51, 52, *52*, 55, 65–68, *67*, 69, 70, 117, 118, 128–33, *129*, 139, 149–50, 152, 160, 166

North Carolina, 23, 26, 27, 89

Ohio, 42, 43, 96, 97

Overman, Lee S., 89

Page, John, 31

Pennsylvania, 21, 29, 141
Perot, H. Ross, 162
Pickering, John, 76
Pierce, Franklin, 11
Pinckney, Charles C., 21
Pinckney, Thomas, 35
Platt, Thomas, 40–42, 105
Plumer, William, 39, 77
Polk, James K., 141, 142
Presidential, disabilities and illnesses, 26, 120–38, 149, 159, 165, 168, 174
Presidential succession, 24–26, 95–119, 164

Quayle, Dan, 46–48, *47*, 137, 159–60, 170

Radical Republicans, 103
Randolph, Edmund, 25
Randolph, John, 76, 80
Reagan, Ronald W., 13, 46, 51, 134–37, 158, 159, 168, 173
Reform, 164–74
Republican party, 40, 42, 43, 44, 46, 53, 66, 67, 69, 85, 89, 102, 109, 114, 117, 119, 124, 128, 132, 149, 152, 163. *See also* Half-Breed Republicans, National Unity party, Radical Republicans, Stalwart Republicans
Rhode Island, 20, 27
Richardson, Elliot, 70
Robertson, William H., 105
Robinson, Joseph T., 92
Rockefeller, Nelson A. 35, 51, 52–53, 119, 139, 154–56, *155*, 157, 158, 165, 173
Roosevelt, Franklin D., 13, 42, 44, 90–93, *91*, 111,

112, 113, 144, 145, 146
Roosevelt, Theodore, 11, 34, 40–42, 47, 85, 86, 95, 107–109, *108*, 110, 124

Scandal, 18, 39, 50, 54–71, 109–10, 159, 165
Selection process, 18, 34–53, 71, 72, 165, 170–72
Senate, U.S., 9, 11, 12, 21, 24, 26, 27, 28, 30, 31, 32, 38, 49, 51, 53, 58, 59, 61, 62, 63, 65, 68, 72, 73, 75, 76, 80, 81, 82, 87–89, 90, 97, 99, 103, 109, 110, 112, 114, 115, 121, 123, 127, 133, 139, 140, 141, 143, 144, 148, 150, 153, 155, 165, 166, 169.*See also* Congress, House of Representatives
Seney, Joshua, 31
Seventeenth Amendment, 105
Seward, William H., 142
Sherman, James S., 11, 43, 73, 86
Sherman, Roger, 21, 22, 24
Shriver, Sargent, 16
Slavery, 45, 62, 80, 99–101, 142, 143
South Carolina, 21, 29, 35, 36, 38, 82, 85
South Dakota, 16, 48
Stalwart Republicans, 43, 105, 106, 107
Stanton, Edwin M., 103
States rights, 82–84, 96, 98
Stevenson, Adlai E. (1835–1914) 43, 120, 121, 123–24
Stevenson, Adlai E. (1900–1965), 43, 45, 65
Stimson, Henry L., 112

206

Stone, Harlan F., 112

Taft, William H., 11, 43, 86
Taney, Roger B., 96
Tariffs, 80, 82, 86, 106, 141, 162
Taylor, John, 58
Taylor, Zachary, 99–100
Tennessee, 46, 62, 102, 160
Texas, 43, 46, 51, 68, 69, 92, 93, 99, 100, 114, 150, 173
Ticket balancing, 43–47, 171, 172
Tompkins, Daniel, 10, 43, 46, 54, 57–60, *60*
Truman, Harry, 12, 13, 17, 42, 65, 95, 111–14, *113*, 147, 148, 167
Twelfth Amendment, 34, 38–39, 40, 61, 165
Twentieth Amendment, 36, 97
Twentieth Century Fund Task Force on the Vice Presidency, 13, 170
Twenty-fifth Amendment, 11, 13, 19, 34, 49, 50, 119, 121, 133–34, 135, 136, 137, 138, 165, 168, 172–74
Twenty-second Amendment, 15, 97
Tyler, John, 11, 45, 95, 96–99, 101, 122, 167

Utah, 100

Van Buren, Martin, 10, 38, 39, 40, *41*, 59, 60, 81, 82, 84, 85, 140–41, 142, 159
Vermont, 38, 107, 110
Vietnam War, 17, 117, 118, 152

Virginia, 21, 24, 25, 26, 31, 35, 43, 76, 80, 96

Walker, Robert J., 97
Wallace, Henry A., 17, 42, 112, 139, 145–47, *146*, 149, 153, 154, 155, 164, 170
War of 1812, 57, 79, 121
Warren, Charles B., 89
Warren, Earl, 115
Washington, George, 15, *22*, 27, 29, 30, 31–32, 43
Watson, James E., 90
Webster, Daniel, 39, 82, 98, 99, 100, 121
Welles, Gideon, 142
West Virginia, 67
Wheeler, William A., 10, 40, 43
Whig party, 39, 44, 96, 97, 98, 99, 100, 101
White, Alexander, 31
White, Samuel, 38
Wilkinson, James, 56
Williamson, Hugh, 23
Wilson, Edith, 126-27, 128, 173
Wilson, Henry, 10, 17, 39, 54, 63–65
Wilson, James, 23
Wilson, Woodrow, 9, 32, 43, 74, 120, 124–28, 130, 173
Wisconsin, 42
Wolff, Jerome B., 70
World War I, 86, 127
World War II, 93, 112, 113–14, 144, 146–47

ABOUT THE AUTHOR

BARBARA SILBERDICK FEINBERG graduated from Wellesley College and earned a Ph.D. in political science from Yale University. She is a full-time writer and her recent books for Franklin Watts include: *Harry S. Truman, Words in the News: A Student's Dictionary of American Government and Politics, American Political Scandals Past and Present, The National Government, State Governments,* and *Local Governments.* She has also written *The Constitution: Yesterday, Today, and Tomorrow,* and is a contributor to *The Young Reader's Companion to American History.*

Ms. Feinberg lives in New York City with her two Yorkshire terriers. Among her other interests are growing African violets and orchids, collecting autographs of historical personalities, and her two adult sons, Jeremy and Douglas.